THE GOOD ON THE DARK WEB

Unveiling the Hidden Potential for Positive Change

Geoffrey Zachary

CONTENTS

Title Page

Part I: Demystifying the Dark Web   7

Chapter 1: History and Origins of the Dark Web - Seeds of   8
Anonymity in the Digital Garden

Chapter 2: Technical Foundations - Delving into the Maze: 11
How the Dark Web Works

Chapter 3: Unveiling the Layers: From Surface Web to Dark   14
Depths

Chapter 4: Myths and Misconceptions Debunked -   17
Navigating the Murky Waters of Perception

Chapter 5: Digital Doubloons in the Shadows - The Role of   20
Cryptocurrencies on the Dark Web

Part II: The Silver Linings   23

Chapter 6: Whispers in the Shadows - The Dark Web as a   24
Haven for Free Speech

Chapter 7: Whispers in the Code: Activism and   27
Whistleblowing - Snowden, Assange, and Beyond

Chapter 8: Shattering the Digital Walls - Bypassing   30
Censorship in Oppressive Regimes

Chapter 9: Whispers of Solidarity in the Shadows - Finding   33
Safe Spaces in Anonymous Support Groups

Chapter 10: Beyond the Canvas - Unfettered Expression in   36
the Dark Web's Depths

Part III: Securing Digital Freedom 39

Chapter 11: Whispers in the Fog - Navigating the Murky 40
Waters of Privacy and Anonymous Browsing

Chapter 12: Safeguarding Voices in the Shadows - 44
Protecting Journalists and Their Sources in the Dar

Chapter 13: Arsenal in the Shadows - Digital Tools for the 48
Modern Rebel: VPNs, Tor, and Beyond

Chapter 14: Sentinels in the Shadows - Cybersecurity 51
Measures and the Dark Web

Chapter 15: Beyond the Walls: Decentralized Platforms and 54
the Dawn of a New Web

Part IV: Unseen Beneficial Activities 57

Chapter 16: Sharing the Light: Open-Source Science 58
Illuminates the Path to Truth

Chapter 17: Whispers of the Past - Archiving the Web's 61
Ephemeral Echoes

Chapter 18: Whispers Across Time: E-books and Rare Texts 64
Archives - Preserving the Written Word in a

Chapter 19: Unearthing Ghosts in the Machine: Rare 67
Software and Abandonware Libraries

Chapter 20: Unearthing Ghosts in the Machine: Abandoned 70
Theories and Discoveries

Part V: Economy and Commerce 74

Chapter 21: Niche Markets and Custom Goods - Navigating 75
the Shadows of Demand

Chapter 22: Freelance Services: Skills Beyond Borders - 78
Where Expertise Meets Anonymity

Chapter 23: Crowdfunding Beyond Traditional Limits - 81
Where Innovation Meets Anonymity

Chapter 24: Whispers of Fairness - Fair Trade and Direct 84
Producer-Consumer Channels

Chapter 25: Navigating the Blackout: Business Continuity 87
in Internet Shutdowns

Part VI: Edges of Morality 90

Chapter 26: Whispers of Rebellion: Digital Vigilantism and 91
Hacktivist Groups

Chapter 27: Whispers Across Worlds: Role-playing and 94
Simulated Worlds

Chapter 28: Whispers of Ethics: Philosophical Debates on 97
Defining Good and Bad

Chapter 29: Whispers of Identity: The Ethics of Digital 100
Anonymity

Chapter 30: Whispers of Harmony: Finding the Balance 103
between Security, Anonymity, and Morality

Part VII: Education and Knowledge 106

Chapter 31: Digital Libraries: Access to Restricted 107
Information

Chapter 32: Whispers of Knowledge: Online Courses and 110
Underground Academia

Chapter 33: Whispers of Collaboration: Communities of 113
Enthusiastic Learners

Chapter 34: Whispers in the Shadows: Navigating 116
Censored Information in Restricted Areas

Chapter 35: Coding Constellations: The Rise of 119
Programming and Tech Skills Platforms

Part VIII: Health and Wellness 122

Chapter 36: Access to Restricted Medication 123

Chapter 37: Whispers of Hope: Mental Health Platforms 126
and Support on the Dark Web

Chapter 38: Whispers of Wellness: Exploring 129
Unconventional Therapies and Remedies on the Dark Web

Chapter 39: Whispers of Support: Navigating Health 132

Forums and Patient Communities on the Dark Web

Chapter 40: Whispers of Hope: Unravelling the Secrets of   135
Rare Diseases on the Dark Web

Part IX: Entertainment   138

Chapter 41: Whispers on the Silver Screen: Exploring   139
Indie Films and Documentaries on the Dark Web

Chapter 42: Whispers of Melody: Unconventional Music   142
and the Dark Web

Chapter 43: Pixels of Nostalgia: Retro Gaming and Mods   145
on the Dark Web

Chapter 44: Whispers of Dissent: Uncensored Voices and   148
Forbidden Narratives on the Dark Web

Chapter 45: Unofficial Fan Content and Creations - Where   151
Passion Meets Copyright

Part X: Humanitarian Efforts   154

Chapter 46: Secure Communication for Human Rights   155
Activists - Whispers in the Shadows, Voices for Ch

Chapter 47: Planning and Organizing Protests   158

Chapter 48: Discreet Fundraising for Just Causes -   161
Walking the Ethical Tightrope

Chapter 49: Reporting Human Rights Abuses   164
Anonymously - Whispers in the Dark, Hope for Justice

Chapter 50: Anonymous Charity - Giving in the Shadows,   167
Shining a Light on Lives

Part XI: Overcoming Challenges   170

Chapter 51: Dark Web's Fight against Child Exploitation   171

Chapter 52: Shining a Light on Darkness - Reporting and   175
Tracking Illegal Activities

Chapter 53: Digital Hygiene: Navigating the Shadowlands   178
Safely

Chapter 54: Legal Labyrinth and Uncharted Horizons -   180

The Future of the Dark Web

Chapter 55: Lessons from Shutdowns: Silk Road and Beyond — 182

Part XII: Understanding Diverse Communities — 184

Chapter 56: Religious Communities under Repression — 185

Chapter 57: Politically Suppressed Individuals and Groups — 188

Chapter 58: Amplifying Voices: Minority Communities and the Dark Web — 192

Chapter 59: Whispers of Heritage: Preserving Endangered Cultures on the Dark Web — 195

Chapter 60: Beacons of Hope: Support Networks for Immigrants and Refugees on the Dark Web — 198

Part XIII: Future Potential — 201

Chapter 61: Glimmers of Light: Advancements in Tor and Privacy Technologies — 202

Chapter 62: The Digital Frontier: Exploring Evolving Economies on the Dark Web — 205

Chapter 63: Whispers of Change: The Future of Digital Activism on the Dark Web — 208

Chapter 64: Uncharted Territory: Ethical Debates and the Next Generation of the Dark Web — 211

Chapter 65: Cultivating Light: Expanding the Positive Aspects of the Dark Web — 214

Part XIV: Personal Stories — 217

Chapter 66: Whispers in the Darkness: An Activist's Diary - A Life Saved by the Dark Web — 218

Chapter 67: From Sceptic to User: A Journalist's Journey into the Heart of the Dark Web — 221

Chapter 68: The Tale of a Dark Web Samaritan: Hope in the Shadows — 224

Chapter 69: Hope in the Shadows: A Whistle-blower's 227
Chronicle

Chapter 70: A Visionary's Dream: Weaving Light into the 230
Dark Web Tapestry

Conclusion: 233

Disclaimer for "The Good on the Dark Web" 236

The Good on the Dark Web

Introduction
Overview of the Dark Web: Beyond the Negative Hype

The Dark Web often carries a negative reputation due to its association with illegal activities, but it's important to understand its broader context and uses beyond the sensational headlines.

What is the Dark Web?

The Dark Web is a part of the internet that is not indexed by standard search engines like Google or Bing. It requires specific software, configurations, or authorization to access, with the most common tool being the Tor browser, which anonymizes users' locations and usage.

Beyond Illegal Activities

While it's true that the Dark Web can be used for illegal transactions, such as the sale of drugs, weapons, and stolen data, it also serves legitimate and positive purposes. Here are some of the notable ones:

1. Privacy Protection: For individuals living in countries with strict censorship and surveillance, the Dark Web provides a platform to communicate freely and access information without fear of government retaliation.

2. Secure Communication: Journalists, whistle-blowers, and activists often use the Dark Web to share sensitive information securely, protecting their sources and themselves from potential repercussions.

3. Access to Information: It serves as a repository for a vast amount of information not available on the regular internet, including rare books, uncensored news, and scientific reports.

4. Services and Goods: Beyond illegal goods, the Dark Web also has markets for legal items, including art, books, and rare collectables, providing anonymity for both buyers and sellers.

Challenges and Risks

Despite its positive uses, navigating the Dark Web comes with risks. The anonymity it provides can also shield malicious actors, making users vulnerable to scams, hacking, and exposure to illegal material. Additionally, law enforcement agencies around the world monitor the Dark Web for illegal activities, which can lead to potential legal issues for users, even those with no ill intent.

Ethical Considerations

The ethical considerations surrounding the Dark Web are complex. It raises questions about the balance between privacy and security, the right to free speech versus the need to prevent illegal activities, and the role of government and law enforcement in monitoring internet spaces without infringing on personal liberties.

Conclusion

The Dark Web is a multifaceted part of the internet with both positive and negative aspects. Its role in providing a platform for privacy and free speech cannot be overlooked, despite the challenges and risks associated with its use. Understanding the Dark Web beyond the negative hype requires acknowledging its potential for both harm and good, along with the ethical dilemmas it presents.

Diving Deeper: Beyond the Shadowy Depths of the Dark Web

The internet we know – the sunlit surface where we shop, socialize, and scroll through cat videos – is just an archipelago in the vast digital ocean. Beneath the waves, unseen by most, lies the dark web, a realm shrouded in anonymity and often associated with nefarious activities. But like the ocean floor hiding vibrant coral reefs teeming with life, the dark web holds secrets beyond the sensationalized narratives of cybercrime and illegal markets.

This expedition, dear reader, invites you to shed the preconceived notions about the dark web's shadowy depths. We'll don our metaphorical diving suit, equipped with curiosity and critical thinking, and plunge into this submerged terrain. Brace yourself, for amidst the murky waters, we'll find stories of resilience, innovation, and a fight for freedom in the digital age.

Firstly, let's dispel the myth of a homogenous "dark web." It's not a single, monolithic entity, but rather a network of overlays hidden within the regular internet. These layers operate through anonymizing technology like Tor, which encrypts traffic and routes it through a decentralized network of relays, making it nearly impossible to trace users or websites. This inherent anonymity empowers a surprising diversity of communities and activities.

Whispers of Freedom: Imagine individuals in oppressive regimes accessing uncensored news and sharing stories of dissent. Activists in authoritarian states leverage the dark web to organize protests and evade surveillance. In countries where certain activities are criminalised, communities find safe spaces for these hidden corners become digital havens for the marginalized, allowing them to exercise their fundamental rights to information, expression, and association.

Building Bridges of Knowledge: Beyond activism, the dark web harbours vibrant communities around niche interests and alternative lifestyles. Think of self-taught coders sharing programming tips, hobbyists exchanging rare vinyl records, or even closed communities dedicated to sustainable living practices. These digital enclaves foster collaboration and knowledge sharing, defying the constraints of geography and censorship.

Emergence of the Unbanked: For those excluded from traditional financial systems, the dark web offers alternative solutions. Cryptocurrencies like Bitcoin provide access to financial services for the underbanked and unbanked, empowering individuals to manage their own money without relying on centralized institutions. While concerns about illegal transactions remain, the potential for financial inclusion and innovation in this realm is undeniable.

Innovation in the shadows: Beyond the social impact, the dark web has spurred technological advancements. The need for secure communication and anonymity fostered innovations in cryptography and decentralized technologies. Developments like Tor and blockchain, originally born in the dark web, are now finding applications in legitimate fields like cybersecurity and supply chain management.

However, as with any powerful tool, the dark web's anonymity can be used for harmful purposes. Illegal marketplaces peddle everything from narcotics to weapons, and cybercriminals exploit its shadows to conduct fraud and malware attacks. We must acknowledge these dangers and advocate for responsible development and policing of this digital frontier.

This expedition into the dark web is not an endorsement of all its activities, but rather a call for nuanced understanding. By recognizing the complexities and contradictions within its depths, we can move beyond fear-mongering and appreciate its potential for positive change. Like any ecosystem, the dark web holds both beauty and danger, and it's our responsibility to explore it with a critical eye and a commitment to harnessing its potential for good.

The journey ahead promises many more discoveries. In subsequent chapters, we'll delve deeper into specific stories – from whistle-blowers using the dark web to expose corruption to tech-savvy communities building alternative economies. We'll also examine the challenges and opportunities for law enforcement and policymakers in navigating this murky terrain.

So, adjust your metaphorical mask, dear reader, and prepare to venture further into the dark web. Remember, like any expedition, the true riches lie not just in the destination, but in the knowledge and perspectives gleaned along the way. Let's dive in together, eyes wide open, and see what wonders (and challenges) await in the shadowed depths.

PART I: DEMYSTIFYING THE DARK WEB

CHAPTER 1: HISTORY AND ORIGINS OF THE DARK WEB - SEEDS OF ANONYMITY IN THE DIGITAL GARDEN

The internet, once envisioned as a utopian digital paradise, has evolved into a landscape of both light and shadow. While vibrant forums of communication and commerce thrive on the sunlit surface, an enigmatic realm lurks beneath, known as the dark web. Shrouded in anonymity and often associated with clandestine activities, this hidden network holds a history intertwined with innovation, activism, and a persistent quest for digital freedom.

Our expedition into the dark web begins not in the murky depths of illegality, but in the fertile soil of technological advancement. The roots of its existence stretch back to the 1960s, with ARPANET, the precursor to the internet, initially designed for secure communication within the U.S. Department of Defence. This focus on secure, anonymous networks planted the first seeds of what would later blossom into the dark web.

The next crucial growth spurt came in the 1970s, with the invention of packet switching by Leonard Kleinrock at UCLA. This ground-breaking technology paved the way for decentralized data transmission, a key cornerstone of anonymity in the future dark web. Think of it as creating a network of unlabelled paths through a forest, allowing information to travel without revealing its origin or destination.

Then came the 1980s, and with it, the birth of Freenet, an early anonymizing network conceived by Ian Clarke. Freenet used a peer-to-peer architecture, further distancing users from potential surveillance by distributing data across a network of interconnected computers. Imagine whispers shared between thousands of trees, their rustling leaves obscuring the source of the sound.

But the true catalyst for the dark web's emergence arrived in the early 2000s with the creation of Tor by the U.S. Naval Research Laboratory. This software revolutionized online anonymity by employing an "onion routing" system. Imagine information wrapped in multiple layers of encryption, like an onion with each peel obscuring its hidden core. By bouncing data through a global network of volunteer relays, Tor effectively masked users' locations and browsing activities, enabling the dark web to bloom in its full shadowy glory.

The initial inhabitants of this newfound digital haven were not nefarious actors, but dissidents and activists seeking escape from oppressive regimes. Journalists in countries with strict censorship laws found a platform to share the truth beyond the reach of government censors. Activists in authoritarian states leveraged the dark web to organize protests and evade surveillance, their whispers becoming amplified echoes of resistance.

However, as with any fertile land, the dark web also attracted opportunistic weeds. Illegal marketplaces began to sprout, offering everything from pirated software to illicit drugs. Cybercriminals saw the potential for anonymity and exploited it for their nefarious activities, casting a long shadow over the dark web's narrative.

This intricate mix of positive and negative uses continues to define the dark web's landscape. As we move forward in our exploration, we'll delve deeper into these contrasting roles, examining the stories of whistle-blowers using the dark web to expose corruption, the communities building alternative economies, and the ongoing struggle against illicit activities within this enigmatic digital territory.

Remember, like any garden, the dark web requires careful tending. By understanding its history and origins, we can better navigate its complexities and cultivate the potential for positive change within its depths. So, join us as we continue our journey, armed with knowledge and critical thinking, ready to unveil the hidden stories and challenges within the labyrinthine network known as the dark web.

CHAPTER 2: TECHNICAL FOUNDATIONS - DELVING INTO THE MAZE: HOW THE DARK WEB WORKS

We've glimpsed the historical roots of the dark web, now it's time to descend deeper, past the sunlit meadows of basic understanding, into the labyrinthine realm of its technical operation. Buckle up, dear reader, as we explore the gears and pulleys that keep this veiled network humming, from anonymity-preserving protocols to hidden doors and secret passages.

The key to understanding the dark web lies in its architecture, a stark contrast to the open highways of the regular internet. Imagine a maze instead, its twisting paths obscuring your location and destination. In this analogy, the walls are built with layers of encryption, each scrambling your data like a medieval cypher before passing it on.

The primary tool for constructing this labyrinth is Tor, the software that powers most dark web access. Think of Tor as a series of tunnels, each manned by a trusted guardian who peels off a layer of encryption before sending the information on to the next tunnel. By the time it reaches its final destination, your data is so thoroughly disguised that pinpointing its origin becomes nearly impossible.

But anonymity isn't the only tool in the dark web's arsenal. Websites known as "onion sites" form the hidden nodes within the maze. These websites have special addresses ending in ".onion," accessible only through Tor. Imagine them as secret doors tucked away in the maze walls, leading to hidden chambers accessible only to those who are privy to the location and access code.

Once inside these onion sites, you'll encounter a diverse landscape. Some resemble marketplaces, but instead of clothes and gadgets, they offer contraband and illicit services. Others function as forums for niche communities, from crypto enthusiasts to political dissidents. Think of them as hidden rooms within the maze, each buzzing with conversation and activity tailored to specific interests.

Navigating this shadowy network requires caution and knowledge. Special search engines, like DuckDuckGo and Grams, cater to the dark web, indexing onion sites and enabling basic searches. But unlike Google, these tools operate in the shadows, their algorithms shrouded in secrecy. Think of them as cryptic maps, offering rough directions but demanding keen navigational skills and a healthy dose of scepticism.

However, the technical wizardry of the dark web isn't fool proof. Law enforcement agencies have developed their tools for traversing the maze, occasionally catching glimpses of the shadows within. And while anonymity protects users, it can also embolden criminal activity. Think of the darkness amplifying whispers, both virtuous and malicious, in equal measure.

As we move forward in our exploration, we'll delve deeper

into specific technical aspects – from the vulnerabilities within encryption to the challenges faced by law enforcement. We'll also shed light on the tools and resources available to navigate the dark web safely and responsibly.

Remember, dear reader, venturing into the dark web requires more than just technical expertise. It demands critical thinking, awareness of potential dangers, and an understanding of the ethical complexities that lurk within its shadows. Only with such preparation can we truly appreciate the potential and the perils this enigmatic digital realm holds. So, let's continue our journey together, armed with knowledge and caution, ready to chart a safe and insightful path through the hidden corners of the dark web.

CHAPTER 3: UNVEILING THE LAYERS: FROM SURFACE WEB TO DARK DEPTHS

As we delve deeper into the digital ocean, dear reader, it's crucial to equip ourselves with a map. For beneath the familiar surface of the internet lies a complex ecosystem, with distinct layers housing diverse denizens and activities. Today, we embark on a cartographic expedition, charting the treacherous waters of the surface web, the hidden depths of the deep web, and the shadowy abyss of the dark web.

The Surface Glimmer: Imagine the surface web as a bustling marketplace, sunlit and brimming with familiar sights. Here, we shop online, socialize through social media, and consume news from mainstream sources. It's the internet we know and love, readily accessible through Google searches and conventional browsers. Its inhabitants are diverse – from online retailers and bloggers to news outlets and government websites. Think of it as the brightly lit coral reefs teeming with colourful fish, easily observed, and documented.

The Deep Dive: Descending beyond the surface shimmer, we encounter the vast expanse of the deep web. Unlike its sunlit counterpart, the deep web remains hidden from search engines like Google, shrouded in a veil of anonymity. But this isn't a realm of nefarious activity; it's a treasure trove of hidden content, accessible only through specific links or credentials.

Picture the deep web as a network of underwater caves, each holding unique secrets. These caves house personal email accounts, online banking portals, subscription-based services like Netflix, and university databases. While not inherently illegal, the information within these caves is private, requiring authorization to enter. Think of it as the silent, bioluminescent creatures of the deep sea, unseen by most but vital to the ocean's health.

The Shadowy Abyss: As we navigate deeper, the water grows colder and the light fades. Here lies the dark web, an enigmatic network shrouded in anonymity and often associated with illegal activities. Accessed through specialized software like Tor, the dark web operates like a hidden archipelago, its islands harbouring marketplaces for contraband, encrypted communication platforms for whistle-blowers, and forums for niche communities.

Think of the dark web as the ocean's deepest trenches, home to both fascinating creatures and perilous dangers. This realm attracts hackers and cybercriminals seeking anonymity for their illicit activities, alongside activists and dissidents fighting for freedom in oppressive regimes. The line between good and bad blurs here, demanding cautious exploration and critical thinking.

But distinguishing these layers isn't always straightforward. The boundaries are fluid, with websites sometimes straddling multiple depths. A social media platform, for instance, might reside on the surface but offer private messaging features accessible only through the deep web. Similarly, a dark web marketplace might host links to legitimate news articles, inadvertently connecting the shadows to the sunlight.

It's crucial to remember that these layers aren't isolated ecosystems. Information flows between them, carried by currents of data. News travels from the surface to the deep web through email chains and online forums. Whistle-blowers on the dark web leak information that surfaces in headlines, exposing corruption and sparking change. In this interconnected ecosystem, understanding each layer empowers us to navigate the whole with greater awareness and responsibility.

As we move forward in our exploration, we'll delve deeper into each layer, examining the stories of individuals navigating its complexities. We'll meet hackers risking their freedom to expose vulnerabilities, librarians building knowledge databases within the deep web, and activists using the dark web to fight for human rights.

Throughout our journey, let's remain mindful that these online depths, like any wilderness, demand respect and caution. By equipping ourselves with knowledge, critical thinking, and a sense of ethical responsibility, we can navigate the darkness and discover the unexpected treasures hidden within the layers of the web. So, reader, adjust your digital scuba gear and hold tight, for our expedition into the heart of the internet continues!

CHAPTER 4: MYTHS AND MISCONCEPTIONS DEBUNKED - NAVIGATING THE MURKY WATERS OF PERCEPTION

As we've plunged into the depths of the dark web, dear reader, we've encountered a complex and often misunderstood realm. But navigating this enigmatic territory requires not just knowledge, but also dismantling the fog of misconceptions that shrouds it. So, prepare your metaphorical diving bell, for we're diving into the murky waters of myth and misconception surrounding the dark web, dispelling its shadows with the torch of truth.

Myth #1: The Dark Web is a Monolithic Entity: Imagine a map labelling the ocean as a single, homogenous landmass. That's how inaccurate this myth is. The dark web is not a single space, but rather a constellation of hidden networks and websites, each with its purpose and audience. It's as diverse as the creatures of the deep sea, encompassing vibrant communities, niche forums, and, yes, even illegal marketplaces. To lump them all together is like claiming all forests are haunted simply because some harbour ancient legends.

Myth #2: Everything on the Dark Web is Illegal: While the dark web's anonymity attracts criminal activity, it's not synonymous with illegality. Think of it as a tool available to both good and bad actors. It's used by journalists in oppressive regimes to share the truth, by activists to organize protests, and by libraries to build digital archives of censored material. Just like a hammer can build a house or break a window, the dark web's purpose depends on the hands wielding it.

Myth #3: Anyone can Access the Dark Web: Contrary to popular belief, accessing the dark web isn't a black magic ritual reserved for seasoned hackers. While it requires specialized software like Tor, the process is akin to learning a new language. Tools and guides are readily available online, offering instructions and support for safe and responsible exploration. Think of it as learning to dive with scuba gear – preparation and knowledge are key, but it's not an exclusive club accessible only to the elite.

Myth #4: You're Completely Anonymous on the Dark Web: Anonymity on the dark web is a spectrum, not a guarantee. While Tor provides valuable layers of protection, it's not infallible. Law enforcement agencies have developed their tools for tracing activity, and careless users can unwittingly reveal their information. Think of it as wearing camouflage in the jungle – it makes you harder to find but doesn't erase your presence.

Myth #5: The Dark Web is a Hacker Haven: While hackers utilize the dark web's anonymity for their exploits, they're not the sole inhabitants. Think of it as a busy city square – you'll find street performers, protesters, vendors, and, yes, the occasional pickpocket. But to focus solely on the pickpockets would paint a wildly inaccurate picture of the square's vibrant life.

Debunking these myths is crucial for understanding the dark web's true potential. It's not a monster lurking beneath the surface, but a complex ecosystem with the capacity for both good and bad. Recognizing this nuance allows us to approach it with both caution and curiosity, navigating its depths with informed awareness and a commitment to harnessing its potential for positive change.

As we continue our expedition, we'll encounter real-life stories that challenge these misconceptions. We'll meet librarians building digital havens for censored information, journalists using the dark web to expose corruption, and even entrepreneurs utilizing its anonymity to develop alternative economies. Through these diverse perspectives, we'll paint a more accurate picture of the dark web, one that transcends sensationalized headlines and reveals its potential as a tool for empowerment, innovation, and even social change.

So, reader, adjust your metaphorical diving mask and prepare to see the dark web in a new light. By navigating the murky waters of misconception, we can chart a course towards a deeper understanding of this enigmatic realm, appreciating its complexities and unlocking its potential for good. Remember, with knowledge as our compass and critical thinking as our anchor, we can explore the dark web's depths without succumbing to fear or blindly accepting the myths that cloud its true nature. And in doing so, we might just discover a hidden world teeming with unexpected possibilities.

CHAPTER 5: DIGITAL DOUBLOONS IN THE SHADOWS - THE ROLE OF CRYPTOCURRENCIES ON THE DARK WEB

As we continue our descent into the digital depths, dear reader, we encounter a curious currency glinting amongst the shadows – cryptocurrency. These enigmatic tokens, untethered to traditional banks and governments, have become the lifeblood of many dark web communities, sparking excitement, controversy, and a whole lot of questions. So, adjust your metaphorical headlamp, for we're diving into the murky waters of cryptocurrencies on the dark web, exploring their impact and the multifaceted challenges they present.

Firstly, let's dispel the misconception that cryptocurrencies are solely the domain of nefarious actors. Their anonymity and decentralization empower a diverse range of activities on the dark web. Imagine marketplaces buzzing with the trade of legal but controversial goods, like e-cigarettes or rare books, where traditional payment methods might face restrictions or censorship. Think of them as digital doubloons facilitating transactions beyond the reach of conventional oversight.

But the dark web's anonymity also attracts criminal activity, creating a fertile ground for illicit transactions. Imagine stolen credit card details whispered in encrypted forums, their value exchanged through cryptocurrencies like Bitcoin or Monero. These transactions, cloaked in digital shadows, pose a significant challenge for law enforcement, and raise concerns about the dark web's potential to facilitate crime.

However, the story of cryptocurrencies on the dark web is not merely a binary battle between good and bad. Their decentralized nature empowers whistle-blowers and activists in oppressive regimes. Think of journalists, their identities shielded by anonymity, accepting cryptocurrency donations to fund their investigations and expose corruption. These digital doubloons become tools for resistance, fuelling the fight for freedom in the darkest corners of the web.

Moreover, cryptocurrencies are fuelling innovation within the dark web itself. Imagine decentralized marketplaces built on blockchain technology, offering greater transparency and security than their traditional counterparts. These innovative platforms promise to reshape the future of online commerce, both within and beyond the shadows.

Yet, the challenges remain. Cryptocurrency volatility poses risks for both buyers and sellers, and the anonymity facilitating crime also hinders efforts to combat illegal activity. Imagine a treasure chest overflowing with gold, but also harbouring hidden serpents. The potential for good is undeniable, but so are the dangers lurking within.

Navigating this complex landscape requires a balanced approach. While acknowledging the risks associated with cryptocurrency use on the dark web, we must also recognize its potential for positive change. Law enforcement agencies need innovative tools and strategies to tackle illegal activity without stifling technological progress. Individuals venturing into this realm must remain cautious, and aware of the dangers while fostering the responsible use of this new form of digital currency.

As we move forward, we'll encounter stories of individuals utilizing cryptocurrencies for both noble and nefarious purposes. We'll meet activists funding their fight for freedom with digital donations, entrepreneurs building transparent marketplaces on the dark web, and even law enforcement agents developing strategies to track illicit transactions. Through these diverse narratives, we'll gain a deeper understanding of the intricate relationship between cryptocurrencies and the dark web, appreciating both their challenges and their potential for positive transformation.

So, reader, tighten your grip on your metaphorical shovel and prepare to excavate the complexities of cryptocurrencies on the dark web. By carefully sifting through the shadows, we can unearth valuable insights and pave the way for a future where these digital doubloons are used for good, both within the shadowy depths and beyond. Remember, with critical thinking and a commitment to responsible innovation, we can harness the power of cryptocurrencies to illuminate the dark web and empower a brighter future for all.

PART II: THE SILVER LININGS

CHAPTER 6: WHISPERS IN THE SHADOWS - THE DARK WEB AS A HAVEN FOR FREE SPEECH

As we continue our voyage through the murky waters of the dark web, dear reader, we encounter a beacon of hope amid the shadows - the potential for free speech in the face of censorship and oppression. Imagine a hidden library, its shelves stacked with forbidden knowledge, accessible only to those who know the secret entrance. This is the metaphorical landscape of the dark web for many individuals whose voices are silenced in the harsh realities of their worlds.

In countries with restrictive regimes and limited access to information, the dark web becomes a clandestine platform for dissent. Imagine anonymous forums buzzing with discussions on human rights, journalists sharing censored news articles, and activists organizing protests beyond the reach of government surveillance. These shadowy corners become the echo chambers of the silenced, amplifying whispers of resistance into powerful roars that can shake the foundations of oppressive regimes.

Think of a whistle-blower, risking everything to expose corruption, their documents shared through encrypted channels on the dark web. Such acts of courage, shrouded in anonymity, can spark investigations, lead to reforms, and even topple corrupt governments. In this sense, the dark web becomes a weapon wielded by the powerless, a slingshot against the giants of censorship and oppression.

However, the path to free speech in the shadows is fraught with risks. Imagine trolls and bots flooding forums with disinformation, malicious actors sowing discord, and extremists exploiting the anonymity to spread hate speech. Just as sunlight casts shadows, the freedom afforded by the dark web can breed its darkness. Navigating this landscape requires critical thinking and discernment, separating the whispers of truth from the cacophony of lies and hate.

Moreover, the anonymity that empowers marginalized voices also emboldens criminals and extremists. Imagine hate groups recruiting members, drug cartels coordinating illegal activities, and cybercriminals plotting their next attack. This shadow side of free speech poses a significant challenge, demanding a careful balance between protecting legitimate dissent and combating dangerous activities.

Law enforcement agencies face a daunting task in this regard. Imagine searching for a single needle in a digital haystack, their tools and strategies tested by the anonymity and encryption that shield both the voices of the oppressed and the whispers of criminals. Finding this balance requires innovative thinking, collaboration between governments and tech companies, and a commitment to upholding individual rights while protecting society from harm.

As we journey deeper, we'll encounter stories of individuals fighting for free speech on the dark web. We'll meet dissidents in authoritarian regimes sharing their experiences, journalists challenging censorship with digital tools, and even tech developers building platforms that prioritize secure and responsible communication. Through these diverse perspectives, we'll gain a nuanced understanding of the complex relationship between free speech and anonymity in the shadows.

So, reader, grab your metaphorical lantern and prepare to delve into the labyrinthine halls of free speech on the dark web. By shedding light on its challenges and possibilities, we can contribute to a future where everyone, regardless of location or circumstance, has the right to speak their truth without fear. Remember, in the battle for free speech, even the whispers in the shadows can spark a revolution of change.

This is not a journey to condone all activities within the dark web. It is a journey to understand its complexities, acknowledging the potential for both good and bad, and striving to utilize its power for positive change. By harnessing the power of technology responsibly and advocating for ethical communication, we can ensure that the shadows of the dark web become not a haven for darkness, but a stage for illuminating the voices of the silenced and creating a world where free speech truly shines for all.

CHAPTER 7: WHISPERS IN THE CODE: ACTIVISM AND WHISTLEBLOWING - SNOWDEN, ASSANGE, AND BEYOND

As we navigate the shadows of the dark web, dear reader, we encounter figures cloaked in anonymity, their courage echoing through encrypted channels. These are the digital Davids facing digital Goliaths, the whistle-blowers, and activists whose whispers in the code can topple empires and spark revolutions. Let us step into their world, illuminated by the stories of Edward Snowden, Julian Assange, and countless others who chose to shine a light on the darkest corners of power.

Imagine a young intelligence analyst, disillusioned by the vast expanse of government secrets hidden from the public eye. This is Edward Snowden, whose revelations through the dark web platform Wikileaks exposed the mass surveillance programs of the National Security Agency, forever altering the global conversation on privacy and government accountability. His act of digital dissent, while controversial, sparked a wave of activism and ignited public debate, reminding us that sometimes, the greatest acts of courage are whispered not in a crowded public square, but in the quiet hum of a keyboard.

Across the digital ocean, another figure emerges from the shadows - Julian Assange, the enigmatic founder of Wikileaks. His platform became a conduit for a torrent of leaked documents, exposing war crimes, political corruption, and corporate malfeasance. While his methods – and motives – remain disputed, he championed transparency and challenged the notion of state secrets, forcing the world to confront uncomfortable truths and sparking conversations about the ethics of information in the digital age.

But the stories of Snowden and Assange are merely the tip of the iceberg. Countless anonymous whistle-blowers and activists toil in the trenches of the dark web, risking their careers, their freedom, and sometimes even their lives to expose wrongdoing. Imagine journalists in oppressive regimes sharing censored stories through encrypted channels, human rights defenders organizing protests beyond the reach of government surveillance, and environmental activists exposing illegal activities through anonymous tip lines. These whispers in the code become powerful weapons against injustice, their echoes rippling through the digital landscape and demanding change.

However, the path of digital activism is not paved with roses. Governments and corporations wield powerful tools to suppress dissent, silencing voices, and criminalizing whistleblowing. Imagine encryption cracked, digital trails followed, and anonymous identities exposed. The dark web, while offering anonymity, cannot guarantee complete safety, requiring activists to navigate a treacherous landscape where the stakes are high and the price of failure can be severe.

Despite the risks, the fight for transparency and accountability continues to evolve. New technologies like blockchain and decentralized platforms are emerging as tools for secure communication and information sharing, empowering activists, and whistle-blowers in ways never before imaginable. Imagine an immutable ledger of truth, tamper-proof and accessible to all, a beacon of light that even the darkest shadows cannot extinguish.

As we move forward, we'll explore the diverse narratives of whistle-blowers and activists in the digital age. We'll meet hackers exposing vulnerabilities in critical infrastructure, coders building encryption tools for secure communication, and even ordinary citizens using social media to amplify the voices of the marginalized. Through their stories, we'll gain a deeper understanding of the intricate dance between anonymity and accountability, the risks and rewards of digital activism, and the ongoing struggle for a more transparent and just world.

So, reader, adjust your metaphorical antenna and prepare to pick up the faint signals of courage resonating through the dark web. By amplifying these whispers, we can contribute to a future where truth is not shrouded in secrecy, where accountability reigns supreme, and where the darkness becomes a breeding ground not for fear, but for the seeds of positive change. Remember, even the faintest whispers in the code can spark a revolution, and in the hands of determined individuals, the dark web can become a powerful tool for illuminating the path towards a brighter digital future.

CHAPTER 8: SHATTERING THE DIGITAL WALLS - BYPASSING CENSORSHIP IN OPPRESSIVE REGIMES

As we delve deeper into the labyrinthine network of the dark web, dear reader, we encounter a potent weapon wielded against the barbed wire fences of digital censorship – anonymity. In countries where information is choked off and free speech strangled, the dark web becomes a clandestine tunnel, an escape route for the stifled voices of citizens yearning for truth and freedom.

Imagine waking up to a news feed devoid of dissent, an online landscape painted in the colours dictated by an oppressive regime. This is the harsh reality for millions navigating the internet under the tight grip of censorship. Websites are blocked, independent journalists are silenced, and critical perspectives are erased from the digital sphere. But amidst this suffocating darkness, a flicker of hope emerges – the whisper of the dark web.

For activists and dissidents, the dark web becomes a clandestine haven for uncensored information and unfettered communication. Imagine encrypted forums buzzing with discussions on human rights abuses, independent news portals disseminating alternative narratives, and social media platforms connecting individuals fighting for a better tomorrow. These hidden corners become digital sanctuaries, offering a platform for dissent and a lifeline for those yearning for a taste of unfiltered reality.

The tools for breaching the censorship walls are diverse and evolving. Imagine encrypted messaging apps like Signal and Telegram, their whispers travelling through channels invisible to the watchful eyes of censors. Imagine virtual private networks (VPNs) masking users' locations and identities, transforming them into digital phantoms flitting through the shadows of the internet. Imagine secure file-sharing platforms like Onion Share, their digital packages bypassing border controls and carrying precious cargo – banned books, censored documentaries, and the testimonies of silenced voices.

However, the path to accessing these tools and platforms is fraught with challenges. Imagine scrambling to find reliable sources in a sea of misinformation, navigating complex technical setups amidst limited resources, and facing the constant threat of surveillance and detection. For those living under the hammer of censorship, bypassing the digital walls requires not just knowledge but also courage, resilience, and a tenacious spirit.

The fight against censorship isn't solely waged in the shadows of the dark web. Imagine tech companies developing innovative tools to circumvent filters and firewalls, human rights organizations lobbying for internet freedom, and legal challenges aimed at dismantling the infrastructure of online repression. By uniting efforts in the open world and the dark, a formidable force emerges, one capable of chipping away at the digital fortifications of censorship.

As we journey further, we'll encounter stories of individuals defying digital oppression. We'll meet journalists in authoritarian regimes sharing banned stories through the dark web, activists organizing protests beyond the reach of government surveillance, and even ordinary citizens using social media to amplify the voices of the silenced. Through their tales, we'll gain a deeper understanding of the human cost of censorship, the ingenuity employed to bypass it, and the ongoing struggle for a free and open internet for all.

So, reader, arm yourself with knowledge and empathy as we step into this crucial battleground. By shedding light on the tools and tactics of those defying digital censorship, we can contribute to a future where information flows freely, voices are unmuted, and the dark web becomes not a refuge for the oppressed, but a stepping stone towards a world where the walls of censorship crumble and the internet shines as a beacon of truth and freedom for all.

Remember, even the faintest whisper of dissent can reverberate through the digital tunnels of the dark web, shaking the foundations of oppressive regimes and inspiring others to join the fight for a more open and just online world. In the hands of the courageous and the resourceful, the darkness becomes not a foe, but a fertile ground for cultivating the seeds of digital freedom.

CHAPTER 9: WHISPERS OF SOLIDARITY IN THE SHADOWS - FINDING SAFE SPACES IN ANONYMOUS SUPPORT GROUPS

As we navigate the shadowed depths of the dark web, dear reader, we encounter a hidden haven – anonymous support groups. These online communities, shrouded in the cloak of anonymity, offer solace and connection to individuals grappling with a diverse range of challenges, from marginalized identities to stigmatized experiences. Imagine not a sunlit marketplace or a buzzing forum, but a dimly lit room where hushed voices share burdens they cannot bear in the harsh light of the open world.

For individuals navigating ostracized identities, the dark web presents a safe space to connect with others who understand their struggles. Imagine LGBTQ+ individuals in restrictive societies finding solace in encrypted forums, survivors of abuse sharing stories in anonymous chatrooms, and individuals battling mental health challenges exchanging support in hidden corners of the web. These digital sanctuaries offer empathy, acceptance, and a sense of belonging, a stark contrast to the isolation they may face in their daily lives.

The anonymity offered by the dark web is crucial for fostering open and honest communication. Imagine whispers of vulnerability shared without fear of judgment, experiences deemed taboo in the open world laid bare in the safety of encrypted channels. Individuals grappling with addiction, chronic illness, or even unconventional hobbies can connect with a network of understanding, free from the stigma and prejudice that might greet them in their offline spheres.

While these communities offer support and a sense of belonging, they are not without their challenges. Imagine navigating through misinformation and harmful advice in a landscape without centralized moderation. Trolls and malicious actors can exploit anonymity for their gain, spreading negativity and preying on vulnerable individuals. The responsibility for maintaining a safe space therefore falls upon the shoulders of the community itself, requiring a delicate balance between freedom of expression and responsible interaction.

But amidst the potential pitfalls, the stories of healing and solidarity are undeniable. Imagine individuals overcoming addiction with the support of an anonymous online group, survivors of abuse finding the courage to speak their truth, and marginalized individuals discovering a sense of acceptance they long craved. These narratives of empowerment speak volumes about the transformative potential of anonymous support groups within the dark web.

As we journey deeper, we'll meet individuals whose lives have been touched by the power of these hidden communities. We'll encounter LGBTQ+ teenagers finding their voices in encrypted forums, ex-addicts sharing their paths to recovery through online mentorship, and individuals with rare medical conditions discovering solace and resources in anonymous chatrooms. Their stories will reveal the human face of the dark web, not as a breeding ground for criminals, but as a refuge for the ostracized, the isolated, and the vulnerable.

So, reader, shed your preconceptions and allow yourself to be touched by the quiet echoes of resilience resonating through the shadows. By understanding the challenges and the potential of anonymous support groups, we can contribute to a future where technology empowers connection, fosters empathy, and offers a haven for every individual, regardless of their background or their struggles. Remember, even the faintest whispers of solidarity can become powerful waves of change, transforming the darkness of the web into a beacon of hope and support for those in need.

Let us journey forward, not with fear, but with open hearts and minds, ready to explore the unexpected corners of the dark web and discover the communities of courage and compassion that thrive in its hidden depths. For in the shadows, where anonymity reigns, it is often the weakest whispers that carry the greatest strength, reminding us that even in the darkest corners, human connection can illuminate the path towards healing and empowerment.

CHAPTER 10:
BEYOND THE CANVAS
- UNFETTERED
EXPRESSION IN THE
DARK WEB'S DEPTHS

As we traverse our expedition into the enigmatic depths of the dark web, dear reader, we arrive at a vibrant, unexpected vista – a clandestine gallery showcasing artistic expression unleashed from the shackles of censorship and societal constraints. Imagine not a sterile white cube, but a hidden corner of the web humming with music, pulsing with avant-garde visuals, and echoing with poems whispered in defiance of societal norms.

In the shadows of the dark web, artists find a blank canvas unmarred by commercial pressures or political censorship. Imagine musicians uploading experimental tracks free from the constraints of mainstream labels, writers sharing unfiltered poetry that challenges social norms, and filmmakers crafting subversive documentaries on topics deemed too "dangerous" for the open web. This digital sanctuary becomes a fertile ground for artistic exploration, fostering innovation and pushing the boundaries of what art can be.

Anonymity plays a crucial role in this liberation of expression. Imagine artists shedding their real-world identities, their voices detached from expectations and biases. This freedom allows them to tackle sensitive topics, explore controversial themes, and even critique powerful institutions without fear of repercussions. It becomes a space for the marginalized and the dissident to raise their voices, amplifying unheard narratives and challenging established narratives.

While the dark web offers boundless opportunities for artistic expression, it's not a utopian refuge. Imagine navigating through landscapes cluttered with disturbing content, encountering hate speech and violence alongside innovative masterpieces. The lack of centralized moderation demands a critical eye and a healthy dose of discernment as one ventures through this artistic labyrinth.

However, within these challenges lie seeds of community and collaboration. Imagine artists forming anonymous collectives, sharing inspiration and resources in encrypted forums, and co-creating works that transcend individual authorship. The dark web fosters a sense of shared purpose and mutual support, allowing artists to push each other's boundaries and cultivate a unique, underground aesthetic.

As we move forward, we'll encounter stories of artists thriving in the shadows. We'll meet musicians blending political commentary with experimental soundscapes, writers crafting dystopian narratives that critique contemporary society, and filmmakers documenting human rights abuses through immersive virtual reality experiences. Through their journeys, we'll gain a deeper understanding of the potential for artistic expression in the dark web, appreciating its challenges and celebrating its power to provoke, inspire, and even change the world.

So, reader, adjust your metaphorical goggles and prepare to witness the kaleidoscope of creativity pulsing within the dark web's underbelly. By shedding light on this artistic haven, we can contribute to a future where freedom of expression reigns supreme, where artists are unhindered by boundaries, and where the shadows become not a canvas for darkness, but a fertile ground for cultivating the seeds of artistic revolution.

Remember, even the most obscure corners of the web can hold treasures waiting to be unearthed. And in the hands of courageous artists, the dark web can be transformed from a hidden realm into a dazzling gallery, showcasing the boundless potential of human creativity and reminding us that sometimes, the most powerful brushstrokes are those whispering in the shadows.

PART III: SECURING DIGITAL FREEDOM

CHAPTER 11: WHISPERS IN THE FOG - NAVIGATING THE MURKY WATERS OF PRIVACY AND ANONYMOUS BROWSING

In the digital age, the concepts of privacy and anonymity have become as valuable as they are elusive. Amidst the burgeoning surveillance apparatus of states and corporations, the dark web emerges as a nebulous realm where these ideals are both preserved and contested. This chapter, "Whispers in the Fog," delves into the intricate dance of shadows that is privacy and anonymous browsing on the dark web, offering a comprehensive exploration of its mechanisms, implications, and the ethical quandaries it presents.

The Foundations of Anonymity

At the heart of the dark web's allure is the promise of anonymity. This is primarily facilitated by The Onion Router (TOR), a network that routes internet traffic through multiple layers of encryption and random servers worldwide. This process, akin to peeling an onion, ensures that the origin and destination of data remain obscured, earning TOR its name. While TOR is the most well-known, other tools and networks, such as I2P (Invisible Internet Project) and Freenet, also provide similar services, creating a multifaceted ecosystem of anonymous browsing.

Sanctuary in the Shadows

For many, the dark web is a sanctuary. It offers a platform for free expression to those under oppressive regimes, protects whistle-blowers, and shields individuals from invasive tracking and data profiling. This aspect of the dark web highlights the critical need for privacy as a foundation for freedom of speech and thought in the digital era. By facilitating anonymous browsing, the dark web acts as a counterbalance to the pervasive surveillance of the modern world.

The Ethical Maze

However, the shield of anonymity also casts a long shadow. The same mechanisms that protect the oppressed also provide cover for illicit activities, from the sale of illegal goods to the dissemination of harmful content. This duality presents a significant ethical dilemma: how to balance the right to privacy and the need for security. The debate is polarized, with advocates arguing that the benefits of anonymity outweigh the risks, while critics contend that it enables criminal behaviour.

Navigating the Murky Waters

For users, navigating the dark web requires not only technical know-how but also a strong ethical compass. The principles of harm reduction and informed consent are paramount. Users must be aware of the potential risks and take steps to mitigate them, such as using secure and updated software, employing strong encryption for communications, and being discerning about the sites they visit and the information they share.

The Role of Encryption

Encryption is the bedrock of privacy on the dark web. Beyond TOR, end-to-end encrypted messaging services and email providers offer secure channels for communication, free from the risk of interception. This encrypted landscape ensures that even if data is intercepted, it remains unintelligible to unauthorized parties. The importance of encryption in protecting human rights and fostering a free internet cannot be overstated.

The Whispers of Activism and Dissent

The dark web is a testament to the enduring human spirit of resistance. It serves as a digital underground railroad, carrying the whispers of activists, dissidents, and persecuted minorities across digital borders. This chapter highlights stories of courage and ingenuity, from journalists using the dark web to bypass state censorship to LGBTQ+ communities finding safe spaces for expression in countries where they are outlawed.

Privacy as a Human Right

The narrative of the dark web reiterates privacy not as a luxury but as a fundamental human right. In an era where personal data has become currency, the dark web stands as a bastion of resistance against its commodification. This chapter argues for a re-evaluation of privacy in the digital age, advocating for policies and technologies that prioritize individual rights and data sovereignty.

The Future of Anonymous Browsing

As the digital landscape evolves, so too does the battleground of privacy. Advances in quantum computing, artificial intelligence, and surveillance technologies pose new challenges to anonymous browsing. This chapter explores the potential future scenarios, from the arms race between encryption and decryption to the development of new anonymity networks. The resilience of privacy advocates, developers, and users will be crucial in shaping this future.

Conclusion

"Whispers in the Fog" serves as an expedition into the heart of the dark web, revealing it to be a complex ecosystem where the noble and the nefarious coexist. It underscores the importance of privacy and anonymous browsing not just as technical feats but as essential components of digital freedom. As we navigate the murky waters of the internet, the choices we make and the values we uphold will determine the kind of digital world we inhabit. The dark web, with all its contradictions, challenges us to reflect on the kind of future we want to forge in the shadows of the digital age.

CHAPTER 12: SAFEGUARDING VOICES IN THE SHADOWS - PROTECTING JOURNALISTS AND THEIR SOURCES IN THE DARK WEB'S DEPTHS

In the interconnected world of the 21st century, the role of journalism as the Fourth Estate—charged with holding power to account—has never been more critical. Yet, as the digital age progresses, so too do the risks faced by journalists and their sources. This chapter explores the dark web's pivotal role in safeguarding these voices in the shadows, ensuring that the pursuit of truth remains unimpeded by threats of surveillance, censorship, and retaliation.

The Digital Dilemma

The advent of digital journalism has been a double-edged sword. While the internet facilitates the rapid dissemination of information, it also exposes journalists and their sources to unprecedented levels of surveillance. Authoritarian regimes and private entities alike have harnessed sophisticated tracking and hacking technologies, making the confidential communication of sensitive information increasingly perilous. In this treacherous landscape, the dark web emerges as a sanctuary, a place where the free flow of information can continue away from prying eyes.

Anonymity as Armor

At the core of the dark web's utility for journalism is the anonymity it affords. Tools like The Onion Router (TOR) and encrypted messaging apps are not just technical innovations but lifelines for those operating under oppressive regimes or investigating powerful interests. These technologies mask users' identities and locations, making it possible for journalists to research, communicate, and publish without fear of immediate reprisal.

SecureDrop and Beyond

One of the dark web's most significant contributions to journalism is SecureDrop, an open-source platform allowing whistle-blowers to share information anonymously with news organizations. Developed with the express purpose of protecting journalistic sources, SecureDrop has become an indispensable tool in the investigative reporter's arsenal. Beyond SecureDrop, a plethora of encrypted services on the dark web, from email to file sharing, further ensures that sensitive documents can be exchanged with integrity and confidentiality intact.

Case Studies of Courage

The chapter highlights several case studies where the dark web has been instrumental in bringing crucial stories to light. These include exposés on corruption in authoritarian states, revelations of unethical practices within multinational corporations, and the uncovering of global surveillance programs. Each case study underscores the vital role that anonymity and secure communication play in the journalistic process, particularly when confronting subjects who would prefer to remain in the dark.

Ethical Considerations

While the protection of journalists and their sources is paramount, the use of the dark web for journalistic purposes is not without its ethical quandaries. The same anonymity that shields the righteous can also hide the malevolent. The chapter addresses these concerns, emphasizing the importance of ethical guidelines for journalists operating within the dark web. These include verifying information from anonymous sources with the same rigour as traditional reporting and being transparent with readers about the methods used to obtain sensitive information.

Training and Accessibility

The effective use of the dark web by journalists and their sources is contingent upon knowledge and accessibility. Recognizing this, various organizations have initiated training programs on digital security and anonymous browsing techniques. The chapter outlines these resources, including workshops, online courses, and guides, which are crucial in democratizing access to the dark web's protective capabilities.

The Future of Dark Web Journalism

Looking to the future, the chapter speculates on the evolving landscape of digital journalism and the role of the dark web within it. As surveillance technologies become more sophisticated, so too must the tools of anonymity and encryption. The ongoing cat-and-mouse game between journalists and those who wish to silence them will likely intensify, with the dark web serving as a critical battleground in the fight for free expression.

Conclusion

"Safeguarding Voices in the Shadows" illuminates the dark web's critical role in protecting journalism and the free flow of information in an era of digital surveillance. By providing a haven for anonymous communication, the dark web ensures that journalists and their sources can continue to expose wrongdoing and hold the powerful to account. This chapter not only highlights the technical aspects of digital privacy but also celebrates the enduring human spirit of curiosity, courage, and the relentless pursuit of truth. In the depths of the dark web, journalism finds a powerful ally, preserving the light of transparency and accountability in the face of encroaching darkness.

CHAPTER 13: ARSENAL IN THE SHADOWS - DIGITAL TOOLS FOR THE MODERN REBEL: VPNS, TOR, AND BEYOND

As we descend deeper into the enigmatic depths of the dark web, dear reader, we arrive at a hidden armoury – a treasure trove of digital tools meticulously crafted to navigate the shadows and empower modern rebels, activists, and explorers. This is not a warehouse of physical weapons, but a digital arsenal stocked with virtual private networks (VPNs), onion routers (Tor), encrypted messaging apps, and a kaleidoscope of lesser-known technologies, each one a key to unlock hidden doors and bypass digital fences.

Imagine a world where internet access is choked by censorship, information tightly controlled, and dissent ruthlessly silenced. In this landscape, anonymity and secure communication become priceless weapons, and tools like VPNs and Tor transform into shields against digital oppression. Imagine cloaking your online activities in the layered armour of a VPN, its encrypted tunnels channelling your data through a labyrinth of anonymous servers, confounding even the most sophisticated trackers. Or picture yourself sailing the digital seas aboard the Tor browser, its multi-layered encryption bouncing your signal through a global network of relays, leaving only whispers in its wake.

But this digital arsenal is not merely for evading watchful eyes. Imagine journalists unearthing crucial evidence through secure anonymous channels, activists organizing protests beyond the reach of state surveillance, and whistle-blowers exposing corruption without fear of reprisal. These tools become potent instruments for truth-seeking, empowering individuals to challenge the status quo and give voice to the silenced.

However, navigating this technological armoury requires caution and discernment. Imagine stumbling through a maze of obscure settings, grappling with complex configurations, and falling prey to malicious traps hidden within seemingly innocuous tools. Mastering this arsenal demands knowledge, critical thinking, and a healthy dose of scepticism. Not every tool is equally forged, and not every vendor can be trusted.

The quest for anonymity and secure communication is an ongoing struggle. Imagine governments developing ever-more sophisticated surveillance techniques, criminal actors exploiting vulnerabilities in encryption protocols, and tech companies facing a delicate balance between user privacy and national security concerns. Navigating this evolving landscape requires constant vigilance, staying informed about the latest threats and adapting your digital armour accordingly.

As we move forward, we'll encounter stories of individuals wielding these digital tools for a variety of purposes. We'll meet journalists in authoritarian regimes utilizing encrypted messaging apps to communicate with sources, activists leveraging anonymized platforms to organize protests, and even ordinary citizens protecting their digital privacy from prying eyes. Through their narratives, we'll gain a deeper understanding of the practical applications of these tools, the challenges they present, and the ongoing fight for a more secure and open digital landscape.

So, reader, arm yourself with knowledge and prudence as you explore this digital armoury. By understanding the capabilities and limitations of these tools, advocating for stronger online privacy, and demanding ethical development from tech companies, we can contribute to a future where the internet remains a free and open space for exploration, activism, and even rebellion against injustice. Remember, even the simplest digital tools, wielded with courage and intelligence, can become powerful weapons against oppression, illuminating the path towards a world where privacy reigns supreme and the shadows empower, not hinder, the voices of the modern rebel.

CHAPTER 14: SENTINELS IN THE SHADOWS - CYBERSECURITY MEASURES AND THE DARK WEB

As we conclude our expedition into the labyrinthine depths of the dark web, dear reader, we approach a fortified checkpoint – the intersection of cybersecurity and anonymity. Here, whispers of vulnerability brush against the cold metal of digital defences, reminding us that even in the shadows, the spectre of cyber threats looms large. This is not a bustling marketplace or a hidden library, but a fortress bristling with sophisticated weaponry, where cybersecurity measures stand guard against the dark web's lurking dangers.

Imagine not a gleaming shield, but a complex network of firewalls, intrusion detection systems, and malware scanners, their eyes scanning the digital horizon for the faintest flicker of malicious activity. These cybersecurity measures, painstakingly deployed by individuals, businesses, and even entire nations, form the first line of defence against the dark web's denizens, striving to keep our data safe in a world where shadows conceal nefarious intent.

The dark web provides fertile ground for cybercriminals. Imagine stolen data flooding hidden marketplaces, malware disguised as innocent downloads lurking in encrypted forums, and phishing scams crafted with chilling expertise. This digital underbelly presents a constant threat, a playground for those who seek to exploit vulnerabilities and inflict harm. Cybersecurity measures serve as a vital counterpoint, shielding sensitive information, thwarting attacks, and protecting individuals from the dark web's darker side.

However, the battle for cybersecurity is not fought with brute force alone. Imagine not just soldiers on the ramparts, but agile scouts venturing into the shadows, infiltrating hacker forums, and mapping the ever-changing landscape of cyber threats. Dark web monitoring tools become crucial weapons, scanning hidden corners for leaks of stolen data, identifying emerging attack vectors, and providing the intelligence needed to stay ahead of the curve.

The fight for cybersecurity transcends the confines of the dark web. Imagine governments collaborating on international cybercrime treaties, tech companies developing ever-more robust security protocols, and individuals practising good digital hygiene to protect their online lives. This collective effort aims to strengthen our digital defences, making the internet a safer space for all, even as the threats lurking in the shadows continue to evolve.

As we move forward, we'll encounter stories of individuals and organizations navigating the treacherous landscape of cybersecurity. We'll meet IT professionals battling cyberattacks on the frontlines, hackers turned white hats using their skills to counter dark web threats, and even ordinary citizens learning to protect their data and identities in the digital age. Through their narratives, we'll gain a deeper understanding of the complexities of cybersecurity, the diverse threats emanating from the dark web, and the ongoing struggle to keep our online lives safe and secure.

So, reader, equip yourself with a sense of caution and vigilance as you venture through the digital world. By understanding the cybersecurity measures in place, adopting safe online practices, and demanding stronger protections from businesses and governments, we can contribute to a future where the dark web's shadows don't hold dominion over our data and identities. Remember, even the most basic precautions, woven together, can forge a formidable shield against cyber threats, transforming the dark web from a haven for malice into a terrain where security reigns supreme and our digital lives remain our own.

CHAPTER 15: BEYOND THE WALLS: DECENTRALIZED PLATFORMS AND THE DAWN OF A NEW WEB

As we conclude our trek through the murky shadows of the dark web, dear reader, a glimmer pierces the digital horizon - the shimmering utopia of decentralized platforms and services. Imagine not a walled garden controlled by monolithic corporations, but a vast, open terrain where ownership is distributed, data is sovereign, and innovation blooms untamed. Here, whispers of freedom morph into the roar of a revolution, reshaping the very foundations of the internet as we know it.

In this decentralized landscape, power shifts from corporate giants to individual users. Imagine peer-to-peer networks humming with activity, each node a tiny sun in a constellation of collective ownership. Data is stored not on centralized servers, but on a blockchain, an immutable ledger etched across the digital fabric, impervious to manipulation or control. Transactions facilitated not by gatekeepers, but by smart contracts – lines of code whispering agreements that execute with unerring precision.

Decentralization promises a web free from censorship and

discrimination. Imagine artists showcasing their work on unfettered platforms, activists organizing movements beyond the reach of state surveillance, and individuals sharing their stories unburdened by fear of corporate algorithms. This open ecosystem embraces diversity, empowers creators, and grants all voices a platform to be heard.

However, navigating this nascent terrain demands caution and discernment. Imagine stumbling through a tangled jungle of unfamiliar protocols, wrestling with complex interfaces, and falling prey to scams lurking in the undergrowth. Decentralization, while liberating, demands technical savviness and a healthy dose of scepticism. Not all platforms are created equal, and not all promises of freedom ring true.

The road to a truly decentralized web is riddled with challenges. Imagine scalability issues plaguing nascent platforms, malicious actors exploiting vulnerabilities in smart contracts, and the ever-present spectre of centralization creep, where dominant players seek to exert control even in this open territory. Building a secure, robust, and truly democratic web requires ongoing innovation, collaboration, and a vigilant defence against those who seek to exploit its vulnerabilities.

As we move forward, we'll encounter stories of pioneers trekking across this digital frontier. We'll meet developers coding revolutionary protocols, artists carving out independent spaces on decentralized platforms, and communities banding together to build and govern these nascent ecosystems. Through their narratives, we'll gain a deeper understanding of the potential and limitations of decentralization, the challenges of building a web free from corporate control, and the ongoing struggle to shape a future where technology empowers, not subjugates.

So, reader, equip yourself with curiosity and open your mind to the possibilities that shimmer on the horizon. By supporting decentralization efforts, advocating for user-centric technologies, and demanding transparency from the architects of the new web, we can contribute to a future where the internet truly belongs to everyone, not just the privileged few. Remember, even the faintest whispers of innovation, when amplified by the collective voice of a decentralized web, can reshape the digital landscape, transforming the shadows of the old web into a radiant dawn for a more empowering, equitable, and truly free online world.

PART IV: UNSEEN BENEFICIAL ACTIVITIES

CHAPTER 16: SHARING THE LIGHT: OPEN-SOURCE SCIENCE ILLUMINATES THE PATH TO TRUTH

As we conclude our exploration of the hidden depths of the dark web, dear reader, we emerge into the radiant fields of open-source science. Imagine not a clandestine marketplace but a sprawling bazaar of knowledge, where scientific findings, data, and methodologies are freely shared, exchanged, and built upon, illuminating the path to collective understanding. Here, whispers of discovery morph into a harmonious chorus of collaboration, accelerating the pace of research and democratizing access to the frontiers of knowledge.

In the realm of open-source science, collaboration transcends geographical and institutional boundaries. Imagine researchers from across the globe working together on shared platforms, dissecting data sets in real time, and refining research methodologies in an open dialogue. This collaborative spirit fosters cross-pollination of ideas, accelerates innovation, and ensures that cutting-edge discoveries benefit all corners of the world.

Open access to scientific findings empowers researchers in

resource-constrained settings. Imagine scientists in developing nations accessing the latest research papers, sharing data without exorbitant paywalls, and contributing to global knowledge pools. This open exchange levels the playing field, fostering inclusivity and ensuring that research benefits all of humanity, not just the privileged few.

However, the path to open-source science is not without its challenges. Imagine navigating a landscape littered with proprietary data, competing interests, and a publishing system resistant to change. Traditional academic structures often reward individual prestige over collaborative ventures, creating hurdles for open-source initiatives. Shifting mindsets and dismantling systemic barriers requires continued advocacy, policy changes, and a commitment to open-access principles.

The fight for open-source science is not confined to the ivory towers of academia. Imagine citizen scientists contributing to real-world research projects, collecting data through open-source apps, and participating in collaborative analysis platforms. This democratization of research empowers individuals to become active participants in scientific discovery, blurring the lines between professional researchers and engaged citizens.

As we move forward, we'll encounter stories of visionaries illuminating the path towards open-source science. We'll meet researchers pioneering collaborative platforms, institutions embracing open access policies, and citizen scientists contributing to ground-breaking discoveries. Through their narratives, we'll gain a deeper understanding of the transformative potential of open-source science, the challenges it faces, and the collective effort required to make knowledge a truly shared resource.

So, reader, arm yourself with a spirit of collaboration and a thirst for knowledge. By advocating for open-source platforms, supporting initiatives that break down paywalls, and actively participating in citizen science projects, we can contribute to a future where scientific progress, benefits all. Remember, even the faintest whispers of collaboration, when woven together into a chorus of open-source knowledge, can illuminate the path towards a brighter future for science, where truth transcends borders and the pursuit of understanding binds us together in a global quest for shared wisdom.

CHAPTER 17: WHISPERS OF THE PAST - ARCHIVING THE WEB'S EPHEMERAL ECHOES

As we conclude our descent into the ever-changing depths of the internet, dear reader, a hushed echo drifts back from the past – the whisper of forgotten websites, lost media, and fleeting online trends. Here, in the hushed halls of digital archives, we embark on a final expedition, not to explore new frontiers, but to preserve the fragile tapestry of the web's history. Imagine not a bustling marketplace or a hidden forum, but a vast library stacked with digital snapshots, meticulously capturing the ever-evolving landscape of the online world.

In this silent sanctuary, forgotten websites find refuge. Imagine nostalgic pixelated pages frozen in time, their outdated designs and clunky interfaces whispering tales of the internet's infancy. Blog posts long abandoned by their authors are preserved, their fleeting thoughts and experiences offering a glimpse into the zeitgeist of a bygone era. Even the ephemeral buzz of social media trends is captured, snapshots of conversations and memes echoing long after the likes and shares have faded.

The act of archiving transcends mere nostalgia. Imagine

historians studying the evolution of online discourse, researchers analysing the impact of digital trends on society, and artists drawing inspiration from the forgotten aesthetics of the past. Preserving the web's history equips us to understand the present, its trends and controversies rooted in the fertile soil of yesterday's digital landscape.

However, navigating the treacherous currents of internet ephemerality demands constant vigilance. Imagine websites vanishing at the click of a button, data disappearing into the digital void, and forgotten servers succumbing to the relentless march of technological obsolescence. Archiving becomes a race against time, a perpetual struggle to capture and preserve the ever-shifting sands of the online world.

The fight for digital preservation is far from solitary. Imagine individuals diligently archiving personal websites, libraries dedicating resources to historical websites, and international collaborations safeguarding cultural heritage online. This collective effort builds a web of digital memory, ensuring that the whispers of the past don't fade into oblivion but resonate for generations to come.

As we move forward, we'll encounter stories of individuals and institutions battling against the tide of digital amnesia. We'll meet web archivists meticulously capturing snapshots of websites, digital librarians safeguarding vast repositories of online history, and even ordinary citizens contributing to open-source archiving initiatives. Through their narratives, we'll gain a deeper understanding of the importance of digital preservation, the challenges it faces, and the ongoing struggle to ensure that the web's past isn't lost to the future.

So, reader, equip yourself with a sense of respect for the past and a commitment to preserving its digital echoes. By donating personal archives, supporting library initiatives, and advocating for robust digital preservation policies, we can contribute to a future where the web's history isn't a forgotten whisper but a vibrant chorus resonating across generations. Remember, even the faintest digital snapshots, when woven together, can form a tapestry of collective memory, reminding us that the internet's past shapes our present and holds the seeds for a more informed and interconnected future.

CHAPTER 18: WHISPERS ACROSS TIME: E-BOOKS AND RARE TEXTS ARCHIVES - PRESERVING THE WRITTEN WORD IN A DIGITAL AGE

As we continue our expedition across the dynamic landscapes of the internet, dear reader, we arrive at a crossroads where whispers of the past mingle with the digital hum of the present – the intersection of e-books and rare text archives. Imagine not a bustling marketplace or a hidden forum, but a sanctuary sheltering the written word, from crumbling ancient scrolls to shimmering e-texts, all united in their enduring power to transport us across time and space.

In this haven for the printed page, e-books find refuge beyond the fleeting trends of online platforms. Imagine forgotten digital novels resurrected from outdated formats, their stories once again whispering to readers across generations. Academic publications long out of print are meticulously preserved, their knowledge accessible to researchers and students far beyond the confines of dusty library shelves. Even orphaned e-books, abandoned by publishers and lost in the digital void, are rescued and nurtured, ensuring their voices don't fade into the silent abyss of cyberspace.

However, navigating the treacherous terrain of digital ephemerality presents a formidable challenge. Imagine e-books succumbing to format obsolescence, their data rendered unreadable with each technological leap. Copyright restrictions threaten to lock away valuable knowledge, their digital walls silencing the whispers of the past. And the vast ocean of online content makes it even harder to discover these hidden gems, their voices drowned out by the cacophony of the digital age.

The fight for preserving the written word, in both digital and analogue forms, demands a symphony of collaboration. Imagine libraries spearheading digitization projects, salvaging fragile texts from crumbling pages and breathing new life into them through electronic formats. Researchers and archivists join forces, meticulously cataloguing and indexing e-books, creating a map to navigate the hidden corners of the digital library. And even individual readers play a crucial role, donating personal e-book collections and advocating for open-access initiatives.

As we move forward, we'll encounter stories of individuals and institutions safeguarding the whispers of the past. We'll meet librarians battling copyright restrictions to preserve literary heritage, archivists rescuing e-books from the grasp of obsolescence, and even book collectors sharing their digital hoards with the world. Through their narratives, we'll gain a deeper understanding of the importance of preserving the written word, the challenges it faces, and the ongoing struggle to ensure that knowledge and stories transcend the limitations of time and format.

So, reader, equip yourself with a love for the written word and a spirit of stewardship. By supporting library digitization efforts, advocating for open-access policies, and donating your digital libraries, you can contribute to a future where the whispers of the past resonate clearly, enriching our present and bequeathing a legacy of knowledge and stories to generations to come. Remember, even the faintest scribblings on a fragile scroll or the flickering pixels of a forgotten e-book, when preserved and shared, can weave a tapestry of human experience that transcends the boundaries of time, reminding us that the power of the written word endures, whispering across the ages and illuminating the path to a future where knowledge remains accessible to all.

CHAPTER 19: UNEARTHING GHOSTS IN THE MACHINE: RARE SOFTWARE AND ABANDONWARE LIBRARIES

As we conclude our trek through the labyrinthine underbelly of the internet, dear reader, a forgotten whisper drifts from the recesses of time - the ghost of abandoned software, tucked away in dusty corners of digital vaults. Imagine not a bustling marketplace or a hidden forum, but a forgotten museum curated with relics of the digital age, where obsolete programs and forgotten user interfaces stand frozen in time, whispering tales of the tech world's forgotten eras.

In this sanctuary of software ghosts, once-celebrated programs find refuge. Imagine pixelated word processors from the dawn of computing, their clunky interfaces whispering of simpler times. Games long out of print are meticulously archived, their faded graphics and primitive sound effects transporting us back to the childhood bedrooms where they were first played. Even forgotten operating systems, the lifeblood of bygone hardware, are preserved, their lines of code echoing the evolution of digital landscapes.

The act of preserving rare software and abandonware transcends mere nostalgia. Imagine researchers studying the history of technology, tracing the evolution of user interfaces and programming languages. Vintage game enthusiasts breathe new life into ageing titles, ensuring their pixelated joy continues to entertain new generations. And even artists draw inspiration from the aesthetics of the past, incorporating retro elements into their creations, bridging the gap between the old and the new.

However, navigating the murky waters of software obsolescence demands cunning and resourcefulness. Imagine data formats rendered unreadable by modern machines, encryption keys lost to the winds of time, and physical media crumbling into dust. Resurrecting these digital ghosts requires technical expertise, historical detective work, and a dedicated community of tech enthusiasts willing to breathe new life into the once-forgotten.

The fight for digital software preservation is far from solitary. Imagine libraries and museums dedicating resources to archiving vintage software, individuals donating their collections, and tech companies collaborating to develop emulation tools that bridge the gap between old and new platforms. This collective effort creates a digital Noah's Ark, safeguarding the software heritage of humanity and preventing its relegation to the oblivion of forgotten servers and dusty floppy disks.

As we move forward, we'll encounter stories of individuals and organizations battling against the tyranny of digital obsolescence. We'll meet software archivists meticulously cataloguing abandoned programs, retro gamers hacking their way into forgotten operating systems, and even tech giants revisiting their past, unearthing, and remastering classic software for modern audiences. Through their narratives, we'll gain a deeper understanding of the importance of software preservation, the challenges it faces, and the ongoing struggle to ensure that the history of technology isn't lost to the relentless march of progress.

So, reader, equip yourself with a spirit of curiosity and respect for the past. By donating your software relics, supporting archive initiatives, and advocating for emulation tools, you can contribute to a future where the digital ghosts of yesterday aren't just whispers in the machine, but vibrant parts of our collective memory, reminding us, that technology, like ourselves, evolves but never truly disappears. Remember, even the faintest flicker on an archaic screen or the forgotten command line of an abandoned program, when preserved and understood, can illuminate the path towards a future where the history of technology informs the present and inspires the innovations of tomorrow.

CHAPTER 20: UNEARTHING GHOSTS IN THE MACHINE: ABANDONED THEORIES AND DISCOVERIES

In the ever-evolving landscape of science and technology, the pursuit of knowledge often leads to roads less travelled or abandoned altogether. Chapter 20 delves into the dark web's role as a digital crypt for theories and discoveries that have fallen out of the mainstream's favour or been suppressed by prevailing scientific paradigms. This chapter embarks on an expedition to unearth these "ghosts in the machine," shedding light on the dark web's capacity to preserve and disseminate ideas that challenge conventional wisdom.

Sanctuary for Suppressed Knowledge

The dark web has become a sanctuary for academics, researchers, and independent thinkers who find their work marginalized by the scientific community. It offers a platform free from censorship and the constraints of traditional publication channels, where unconventional theories and discoveries can be shared and discussed openly. This freedom has led to the formation of a vibrant, albeit hidden, intellectual ecosystem where ideas, regardless of their acceptance in mainstream circles, are given a voice.

Case Studies of Forgotten Theories

The chapter explores several case studies of theories and discoveries that have found new life on the dark web. One such theory is the concept of "bioelectricity" in the early 20th century, which posited that electrical currents in the human body play a significant role in physiological processes. Despite initial dismissal, discussions and research into bioelectricity have flourished in dark web forums, leading to renewed interest and experimentation in the field.

Another example highlighted is the exploration of "cold fusion" — a claim of nuclear fusion at room temperature that was widely discredited in the 1980s. On the dark web, however, cold fusion has continued to be a topic of serious discussion and experimentation, with various groups claiming to have made significant breakthroughs, albeit without mainstream recognition.

Digital Archives of Lost Knowledge

The dark web also serves as a digital archive for lost or suppressed scientific documents, research papers, and experiments. This chapter uncovers how researchers use the dark web to access and share rare manuscripts and articles that have been removed from public libraries and databases, preserving the knowledge contained within them. These archives are invaluable resources for those seeking to explore paths not taken or to build upon ideas that were prematurely dismissed.

The Ethical Dilemma

The preservation and exploration of abandoned theories on the dark web raise complex ethical questions. The chapter examines the fine line between fostering genuine scientific inquiry and perpetuating pseudoscience. It discusses the responsibility of the dark web's intellectual communities to vet and critique the theories they explore, emphasizing the importance of maintaining scientific rigor and ethics even in the absence of mainstream oversight.

Challenges of Validation

One of the significant challenges facing researchers on the dark web is the validation and peer review of their findings. Without the structure and recognition of conventional scientific publication, proving the validity of one's work becomes a formidable task. The chapter explores innovative approaches to peer review and validation within dark web communities, including collaborative experiments, open-source research models, and the development of independent, decentralized research organizations.

Impact on Mainstream Science

Despite its fringe status, the dark web's repository of abandoned theories has the potential to impact mainstream science. The chapter discusses instances where ideas rediscovered or further developed on the dark web have gradually made their way into academic discourse and research, challenging, and expanding the boundaries of scientific knowledge.

The Path Forward

In conclusion, "Unearthing Ghosts in the Machine" reflects on the role of the dark web as a crucible for scientific diversity and intellectual freedom. It posits that, amidst the shadows, lies the potential for significant discoveries that could reshape our understanding of the world. As we move forward, the interplay between the hidden corners of the dark web and the illuminated halls of mainstream science may well dictate the pace and direction of future advancements. This chapter calls for a nuanced appreciation of the dark web's contribution to the scientific endeavour, advocating for a future where all ideas, regardless of their origin, are evaluated on the merit of their evidence and the rigor of their reasoning.

PART V: ECONOMY AND COMMERCE

CHAPTER 21: NICHE MARKETS AND CUSTOM GOODS - NAVIGATING THE SHADOWS OF DEMAND

Delving deeper into the murky depths of the dark web, we encounter a labyrinth of specialized marketplaces, catering to a diverse and often surprising clientele. Unlike the surface web's sprawling shopping malls, these digital bazaars operate in the shadows, their wares hidden from casual browsers. Here, niche markets flourish, fuelled by anonymity and the desire for goods and services deemed illegal, unethical, or simply unavailable elsewhere.

Our expedition begins with the "hidden Wiki," a network of encrypted websites accessible only through anonymized browsers like Tor. Within this veiled landscape, niche communities dedicated to specific interests congregate. Imagine a clandestine library, each shelf teeming with forbidden knowledge: hacking tutorials, pirated software, financial fraud guides, and even marketplaces devoted to specific illegal items like drugs, weapons, or even endangered species.

But the dark web isn't solely a haven for criminal activity. Many individuals seek anonymity for legitimate reasons, such as journalists operating under oppressive regimes or whistle-blowers exposing corporate wrongdoing. Additionally, specialized marketplaces cater to unique and legal demands, often overlooked by mainstream retailers.

Take, for instance, the vibrant community of collectors seeking rare historical documents, vintage memorabilia, or obscure artistic creations. Auction houses on the dark web offer such items, ensuring confidentiality for both buyers and sellers who may fear public scrutiny. Similarly, niche markets cater to medical or recreational drug users seeking specific strains or alternative medicine treatments unavailable through legal channels, albeit with inherent risks and ethical considerations.

One intriguing aspect of the dark web is the prevalence of custom goods and services. Skilled individuals offer their expertise in areas like hacking, identity theft, or even creating deepfakes – manipulated videos intended to deceive. This raises both ethical concerns and questions about accountability in a realm shrouded in anonymity.

However, within this ethical grey area, there exist individuals offering legitimate custom services. Programmers create bespoke software solutions, writers ghost-write personalized content, and graphic designers craft unique logos for clients seeking discretion. Such services highlight the versatility of the dark web, beyond the sensationalized narratives of criminality.

Navigating these niche markets requires caution and vigilance. Transactions often involve cryptocurrencies like Bitcoin, adding an element of risk due to their volatility and potential for scams. Moreover, the anonymity offered by the dark web attracts unscrupulous actors, making research and verification crucial before engaging in any transaction.

As we venture further, we encounter the murky world of escrow services, platforms designed to mediate transactions on the dark web. These services hold funds in escrow until both buyer and seller confirm satisfaction, aiming to mitigate the risk of fraud. However, their reliability and legality vary greatly, and relying on them necessitates an even deeper understanding of the involved parties and potential risks.

Ultimately, the realm of niche markets and custom goods on the dark web presents a paradoxical landscape. While harbouring illegal activities and ethical dilemmas, it also provides a platform for legitimate, albeit unconventional, transactions and caters to diverse needs beyond the reach of mainstream markets. Approaching this realm with caution, awareness, and a critical eye allows us to glimpse the multifaceted nature of this hidden digital ecosystem.

CHAPTER 22: FREELANCE SERVICES: SKILLS BEYOND BORDERS - WHERE EXPERTISE MEETS ANONYMITY

Our exploration of the dark web takes a turn towards human capital, venturing into the realm of freelance services. This hidden marketplace connects skilled individuals with clients seeking expertise in areas often deemed unconventional or even taboo. Here, anonymity reigns supreme, erasing geographical borders and traditional employment models, while simultaneously raising questions about legality, security, and ethical boundaries.

Imagine a bustling bazaar, its stalls overflowing not with tangible goods, but with whispers of expertise. Hackers offer penetration testing services, writers craft persuasive phishing emails, and graphic designers create counterfeit documents. While such offerings raise immediate ethical concerns, the reality paints a more nuanced picture.

Many legitimate freelancers utilize the dark web's anonymity to protect their identities or bypass restrictions imposed by their countries. Journalists operating under oppressive regimes seek ghost-writers to anonymously publish their work, whistle-blowers expose corporate wrongdoing through hidden channels, and even activists leverage cyber skills to combat censorship or surveillance.

But the line between legitimate and illicit activity blurs easily. Individuals with specialized skills, from lockpicking to social engineering, offer their services to clients with dubious intentions. This raises concerns about the potential misuse of such expertise and the ethical responsibility of both service providers and clients.

Beyond legality, security risks abound. Transactions often rely on cryptocurrencies, susceptible to scams and price fluctuations. Anonymity, while empowering, also poses challenges in verifying the reliability and intentions of both parties. Reputational systems exist, but their accuracy and trustworthiness vary greatly.

Amidst these complexities, legitimate and valuable freelance services exist. Programmers offer custom software development, web designers create anonymous websites for whistle-blower platforms, and data analysts provide insights hidden from public scrutiny. This highlights the potential of the dark web to connect skilled individuals with clients seeking expertise beyond the reach of traditional channels.

One fascinating aspect of this hidden marketplace is the emergence of specialized skills unique to the dark web. Individuals offer expertise in dark web navigation, security measures, and even cryptocurrency laundering, raising additional ethical and legal questions about the facilitation of potentially illegal activities.

As we tread deeper, we encounter escrow services, and platforms aiming to mitigate transaction risks by holding funds until both parties are satisfied. However, their legitimacy and effectiveness vary drastically, and relying on them requires meticulous research and a keen understanding of the involved parties.

Ultimately, the realm of freelance services on the dark web presents a double-edged sword. While harbouring risks and ethical dilemmas, it also fosters a unique ecosystem connecting individuals with unconventional skills and clients seeking expertise beyond mainstream limitations. Approaching this realm with caution, awareness of potential risks, and a strong moral compass are crucial to navigating its complexities and reaping its potential benefits ethically.

CHAPTER 23: CROWDFUNDING BEYOND TRADITIONAL LIMITS - WHERE INNOVATION MEETS ANONYMITY

Our expedition through the shadows of the dark web unveils an unexpected facet: the realm of crowdfunding. Imagine a hidden bazaar, its coffers not overflowing with coins, but with whispered promises and anonymous contributions. Here, individuals and groups bypass traditional fundraising models, seeking support for ventures deemed controversial, unconventional, or even illegal on the surface web.

However, before venturing deeper, let us dispel a misconception: not all dark web crowdfunding falls into the realm of criminality. Many utilize its anonymity for legitimate reasons, seeking funding for causes deemed sensitive or controversial in their societies. Imagine: journalists raising funds to expose corruption, activists crowdfunding legal efforts against oppressive regimes, or whistle-blowers seeking resources to bring wrongdoing to light.

Yet, the shadows also harbour ventures pushing the boundaries of legality and ethics. Groups raising funds for hacking operations, individuals crowdfunding for illegal activities, or even extremists seeking financial support for their agendas paint a darker picture. Navigating this complex landscape requires discernment and an understanding of the potential risks involved.

But the story unfolds further. Beyond ethical considerations, the dark web's anonymity poses unique challenges and opportunities for crowdfunding campaigns. Traditional platforms rely on centralized servers and regulations, often imposing restrictions on campaign content or beneficiary qualifications. The dark web, however, operates decentralized, offering unfettered access to funding but lacking built-in oversight and accountability.

Here, trust becomes paramount. Platforms often leverage escrow services, holding funds until campaign goals are met and promises are fulfilled. However, the reliability and security of these services vary greatly, demanding due diligence from potential contributors. Additionally, anonymity necessitates alternative methods of verifying campaign legitimacy, often relying on peer review and community reputation within specific dark web spaces.

Despite the inherent risks, innovative and legitimate projects also flourish. Inventors with radical ideas, artists exploring controversial themes, and even researchers seeking funding for unconventional projects find a platform on the dark web. This highlights the potential for this hidden domain to support cutting-edge innovation and creative expression beyond the constraints of traditional crowdfunding models.

One fascinating aspect of this realm is the emergence of "dark DAOs" – Decentralized Autonomous Organizations utilizing blockchain technology for crowdfunding and community governance. These self-governing structures raise promising possibilities for transparent and equitable funding distribution but also introduce complex legal and technological questions.

As we venture further, we encounter unique challenges. Transactions primarily rely on cryptocurrencies, susceptible to volatility and scams. The decentralized nature of the dark web makes law enforcement complex, further emphasizing the need for individual responsibility and risk assessment before contributing to any campaign.

Ultimately, crowdfunding on the dark web presents a paradox. While harbouring risks and ethical dilemmas, it offers a platform for unconventional ventures, fosters innovation beyond traditional limitations, and empowers individuals seeking funding outside the mainstream. Approaching this realm with caution, a critical eye, and a strong moral compass is crucial to navigating its complexities and harnessing its potential for good.

CHAPTER 24: WHISPERS OF FAIRNESS - FAIR TRADE AND DIRECT PRODUCER-CONSUMER CHANNELS

As we conclude our expedition through the labyrinthine depths of the dark web, dear reader, a beacon of ethical commerce shines through the shadows – the realm of fair trade and direct producer-consumer channels. Imagine not a bustling marketplace or a hidden forum, but a bustling bazaar where empowered producers connect directly with conscious consumers, weaving a tapestry of economic justice and sustainable practices. Here, whispers of exploitation transform into a chorus of empowerment, echoing across borders and forging a path towards a more equitable global market.

In this ethical marketplace, fair trade principles reign supreme. Imagine farmers receiving fair prices for their labour, artisans rewarded for their craftsmanship, and communities thriving on sustainable practices. No longer subject to the exploitative middlemen of traditional supply chains, producers control their destinies, setting prices, defining working conditions, and reaping the rewards of their dedication. Consumers, armed with knowledge and fuelled by a desire for social responsibility, make informed choices, empowering producers and contributing to a more just and sustainable global economy.

However, navigating the murky waters of ethical trade demands discerning eyes and unwavering commitment. Imagine counterfeit fair trade products flooding the market, misleading consumers, and exploiting genuine efforts. Complex certification processes can prove daunting for small producers, while established giants sometimes mimic fair trade practices without upholding their core values. Vigilant research, critical consumerism, and support for transparent, independent certification bodies are crucial weapons in the fight against greenwashing and ensuring true impact.

The quest for ethical commerce transcends fair trade labels. Imagine vibrant online platforms connecting producers and consumers directly, eliminating exploitative middlemen and empowering both parties. Local farmer's markets flourish, bustling with fresh produce and handcrafted goods, fostering community resilience, and reducing carbon footprints. Peer-to-peer platforms empower artists and creatives, allowing them to showcase their work and connect directly with their audience, bypassing exploitative galleries and studios.

However, building robust direct producer-consumer channels faces challenges. Imagine logistical hurdles hampering access to distant markets, technological barriers hindering online participation, and limited consumer awareness hindering market reach. Collaborative efforts are key – fostering digital literacy among producers, building robust online platforms, and advocating for policies that support local economies and sustainable trade practices are essential steps in creating a more equitable economic landscape.

As we move forward, we'll encounter stories of individuals and organizations blazing a trail towards ethical commerce. We'll meet fair trade pioneers breaking free from exploitative chains, visionary entrepreneurs building innovative direct-to-consumer platforms, and passionate consumers driving the demand for responsible products and practices. Through their narratives, we'll gain a deeper understanding of the transformative potential of fair trade and direct producer-consumer channels, the challenges they face, and the ongoing struggle to build a global economy that values people and the planet over profit.

So, reader, arm yourself with a discerning eye and a commitment to fairness. By supporting authentic fair trade products, seeking out locally sourced goods, and advocating for transparency in the marketplace, you can contribute to a future where whispers of exploitation are replaced by the roar of ethical commerce, empowering producers, rewarding responsible practices, and building a more just and sustainable world for all. Remember, even the smallest purchase made with awareness can ripple through the global marketplace, echoing a powerful message of change and reminding us that the power to create a more ethical future lies in the hands of informed and empowered consumers like you.

CHAPTER 25: NAVIGATING THE BLACKOUT: BUSINESS CONTINUITY IN INTERNET SHUTDOWNS

Our exploration of the internet's shadowy depths concludes, dear reader, not with a whispered secret but with a booming silence – the chilling reality of internet shutdowns. Imagine not a bustling marketplace or a hidden forum, but a city plunged into darkness, businesses shuttered, and communication channels severed. In this unsettling landscape, the whispers transform into panicked sighs, highlighting the fragility of our digital dependence and the crucial need for business continuity plans.

In this digital blackout zone, businesses scramble to adapt. Imagine e-commerce platforms facing lost revenue, news outlets struggling to inform the public, and even emergency services facing communication hurdles. The ripple effects can be devastating, impacting not just financial well-being but also public safety and democratic principles. But amidst the darkness, resilience flickers. Businesses that planned for the unthinkable rise to the challenge, their continuity plans acting as lighthouses guiding them through the digital storm.

The challenges are manifold. Imagine relying on offline alternatives often outdated or inefficient. Communication breakdowns with customers and partners create confusion and anxiety. Maintaining operations and employee morale in the face of uncertainty presents its own set of hurdles. Yet, through innovative solutions and proactive planning, businesses can navigate the storm, emerging stronger and more resilient.

The first line of defence lies in preparation. Imagine conducting risk assessments, identifying critical online functionalities, and outlining alternative communication channels. Exploring offline alternatives, from brick-and-mortar stores to local radio broadcasts, becomes crucial. Secure, offline data backups provide a lifeline in case of digital blackouts. Investing in communication tools with offline capabilities and training employees in alternative methods ensures a semblance of normalcy even in the dark.

Collaboration is key. Imagine businesses partnering with local communities, authorities, and other organizations to share information and resources. Establishing communication channels with key stakeholders, including customers, suppliers, and employees, helps maintain trust and minimize disruption. Collective action can amplify voices and increase pressure on those responsible for shutdowns.

Technology offers solutions too. Imagine encrypted messaging apps providing secure communication channels. Mesh networks and satellite internet, where available, offer alternative online access. Decentralized solutions and blockchain technology provide greater digital autonomy, reducing reliance on single points of failure. While not fool proof, these technological tools can empower businesses to weather the storm.

However, navigating the complexities of internet shutdowns

demands a nuanced approach. Imagine balancing the need for business continuity with ethical considerations. Engaging in peaceful protests and advocating for open internet access is crucial, but avoiding illegal activities and respecting local laws are paramount. Working within the legal framework, while challenging restrictions, ensures businesses do not become pawns in larger political struggles.

As we move forward, we'll encounter stories of businesses demonstrating remarkable resilience. We'll meet entrepreneurs finding ingenious offline solutions, communities banding together to share information, and organizations advocating for digital rights. Through their narratives, we'll gain a deeper understanding of the importance of business continuity planning, the challenges it faces, and the ongoing fight for an open and accessible internet.

So, reader, equip yourself with a spirit of preparedness and a commitment to open access. By incorporating business continuity plans into your operations, supporting initiatives promoting digital rights, and advocating for responsible Internet governance, you can contribute to a future where Internet shutdowns no longer plunge businesses into darkness but instead inspire resilience, collaboration, and the unwavering pursuit of a brighter, more connected world. Remember, even a single voice raised in the digital blackout can echo far and wide, reminding us that the fight for an open and accessible internet is a collective responsibility, ensuring communication, commerce, and information flow freely, even when the lights go out.

PART VI: EDGES OF MORALITY

CHAPTER 26: WHISPERS OF REBELLION: DIGITAL VIGILANTISM AND HACKTIVIST GROUPS

As we conclude our expedition across the diverse landscapes of the internet, dear reader, we arrive at a crossroads where the whispers of dissent morph into the digital roars of hacktivism. Imagine not a bustling marketplace or a hidden forum, but a shadowy digital battlefield where masked figures wield code as their weapons, blurring the lines between activism and vigilantism. In this electrifying realm, whispers of injustice transform into the cacophony of online protests, raising questions about the ethics and effectiveness of hacktivist tactics.

In this digital warzone, hacktivist groups emerge as the self-proclaimed champions of the oppressed. Imagine Anonymous taking down government websites in response to perceived censorship, or LulzSec exposing corporate corruption through data leaks. Their targets range from oppressive regimes and corporate giants to extremist organizations and hate groups. Their methods, however, are as diverse as their motivations, encompassing everything from website defacements and denial-of-service attacks to data leaks and social media manipulation.

However, navigating the murky waters of digital vigilantism demands a discerning eye and a critical mind. Imagine the collateral damage inflicted on innocent bystanders caught in the crossfire. The legality and ethical implications of hacktivist actions remain fiercely debated, with concerns about censorship, freedom of expression, and the potential for unintended consequences constantly swirling. Is it ever justifiable to attack one wrong with another? Where does activism end and vigilantism begin? These are questions that continue to plague the hacktivist movement.

The challenges extend beyond ethical concerns. Imagine the technical prowess required to execute complex cyberattacks, the ever-evolving nature of cybersecurity measures, and the constant threat of government crackdowns. Hacktivist groups often operate on the fringes of legality, facing constant pressure from authorities and powerful adversaries. Maintaining anonymity, securing resources, and coordinating actions across borders demand a high level of skill, dedication, and a willingness to take risks.

Despite the challenges, hacktivist groups continue to evolve and adapt. Imagine decentralized structures making them resilient to takedowns, sophisticated encryption protecting their identities, and social media platforms becoming tools for mobilization and awareness-raising. The rise of "hacktivist toolkits" lowers the barrier to entry, attracting recruits with varying levels of technical expertise and potentially blurring the lines between activism and malicious activities.

As we move forward, we'll encounter stories of individuals and groups pushing the boundaries of digital activism. We'll meet Anonymous members fighting for online freedom, whistle-blowers exposing corporate malfeasance, and digital human rights defenders battling online censorship. Through their narratives, we'll gain a deeper understanding of the motivations behind hacktivism, the challenges it faces, and the ongoing debate surrounding its ethics and effectiveness.

So, dear reader, equip yourself with a critical mind and a nuanced perspective. By engaging in open dialogue, advocating for responsible online practices, and supporting organizations promoting digital rights, you can contribute to a future where the whispers of dissent in the digital sphere lead not to chaos but to meaningful change, ensuring that technology empowers individuals and communities to fight for justice and a more equitable world. Remember, even a single line of code, wielded with purpose and responsibility, can ignite a digital firestorm, reminding us that the fight for a better future can unfold not just on the streets but also in the hidden corners of the online world.

CHAPTER 27:
WHISPERS ACROSS WORLDS: ROLE-PLAYING AND SIMULATED WORLDS

Our expedition through the vast landscapes of the internet concludes, dear reader, not with a technological marvel or a hidden corner, but with an invitation to step beyond reality itself. Imagine not a bustling marketplace or a dark forum, but a shimmering portal to a world unbound by the constraints of the physical. Welcome to the realm of role-playing and simulated worlds, where whispers of imagination transform into vibrant realities, offering escape, connection, and even glimpses into the unknown.

In this boundless realm, possibilities bloom like exotic flowers. Imagine donning the persona of a valiant knight in a medieval fantasy, a cunning detective unravelling a virtual mystery, or an astronaut exploring the farthest reaches of a digital cosmos. Simulated worlds become canvases for the human imagination, fostering creativity, collaboration, and the exploration of diverse identities. Whether seeking community, escapism, or self-discovery, these digital frontiers beckon with experiences tailored to every desire.

Yet, navigating these immersive landscapes demands a discerning mind. Imagine the potential for addiction, the blurring lines between fantasy and reality, and the challenges of maintaining healthy online interactions. Responsible engagement and critical thinking are crucial tools in ensuring that these simulated worlds remain vibrant playgrounds for imagination, not gateways to escapism or harmful online spaces.

The challenges extend beyond individual responsibility. Imagine the ethical considerations surrounding data privacy, representation, and the potential for online harassment and discrimination. As these simulated worlds evolve, robust social norms and clear ethical frameworks are crucial to ensure they remain inclusive, respectful, and safe havens for diverse communities.

Despite the challenges, the potential of role-playing and simulated worlds remains vast. Imagine educational platforms immersing students in interactive historical simulations, therapeutic applications leveraging virtual environments for anxiety management, and research projects utilizing these spaces to study human behaviour and social dynamics. The applications seem boundless, promising to reshape education, healthcare, and our understanding of the human experience.

As we move forward, we'll encounter stories of individuals and communities pushing the boundaries of imagination and connection. We'll meet game developers crafting meticulously detailed virtual worlds, educators utilizing them for immersive learning experiences, and therapists harnessing their power for innovative healing approaches. Through their narratives, we'll gain a deeper understanding of the transformative potential of simulated worlds, the challenges they face, and the ongoing quest to create digital spaces that enrich, educate, and connect us all.

So, dear reader, equip yourself with a curious mind and a sense of responsibility. By engaging in thoughtful discussions, advocating for ethical frameworks, and promoting respectful online interactions, you can contribute to a future where simulated worlds are not just playgrounds for escape, but vibrant platforms for learning, exploration, and fostering connections that transcend the boundaries of the physical. Remember, even the simplest avatar in a digital world can embody the potential for human connection, reminding us that the boundaries between reality and imagination are often more fluid than we think and that the whispers of possibility can lead us to astonishing experiences across countless worlds.

CHAPTER 28:
WHISPERS OF ETHICS: PHILOSOPHICAL DEBATES ON DEFINING GOOD AND BAD

As we conclude our expedition through the multifaceted realms of the internet, dear reader, we arrive at a crossroads where the whispers of technology, morality, and philosophy converge. Imagine not a bustling marketplace or a hidden forum, but a grand library where timeless questions regarding good and bad echo through the halls, challenging us to define these concepts in a digital age. In this intellectual arena, the whispers morph into roaring debates, grappling with the ethical implications of our online interactions and the evolving boundaries of right and wrong.

In this philosophical labyrinth, diverse perspectives contend. Imagine deontologists arguing for universal moral principles, regardless of consequences, while utilitarians prioritize the greatest good for the greatest number, even if it necessitates questionable tactics. Virtue ethicists advocate for character development and personal responsibility, while proponents of consequentialism focus on the outcomes of actions. These contrasting viewpoints illuminate the complexities of online morality, reminding us that there's no singular, universally accepted definition of "good" and "bad" in the digital sphere.

Further complicating matters, the anonymity and fluidity of the online world blur traditional ethical frameworks. Imagine the ease with which online personas mask true identities, facilitating acts of cyberbullying, online harassment, and even digital impersonation. The concept of "harm" takes on new dimensions – from data breaches and privacy violations to the spread of misinformation and the manipulation of online discourse. Defining and addressing these emerging ethical dilemmas requires critical thinking and a nuanced understanding of the unique challenges posed by the online environment.

However, navigating this ethical maze cannot be done solely through abstract philosophical debates. Imagine the need for concrete solutions and actionable frameworks. Responsible technology design plays a crucial role, incorporating ethical considerations from the outset, and prioritizing user privacy, security, and inclusivity. Robust legal frameworks and regulatory measures are essential to curb harmful online activities and hold individuals and platforms accountable. But ultimately, individual responsibility reigns supreme. Cultivating digital literacy, engaging in mindful online interactions, and advocating for ethical practices are crucial steps in creating a more responsible and equitable online space.

As we move forward, we'll encounter stories of individuals and organizations grappling with these complex ethical dilemmas. We'll meet whistle-blowers exposing unethical practices within tech giants, developers creating technology with social good in mind, and online communities fostering respectful and inclusive environments. Through their narratives, we'll gain a deeper understanding of the evolving nature of online ethics, the ongoing challenges, and the inspiring efforts to build a more ethical and responsible digital future.

So, dear reader, arm yourself with a critical mind and a commitment to open dialogue. By participating in discussions about online ethics, promoting responsible technology development, and holding yourself and others accountable for online actions, you can contribute to a future where technology serves as a force for good, empowering individuals and communities to navigate the digital world with ethical awareness and responsible engagement. Remember, even a single voice raised in pursuit of ethical practices can spark a ripple effect, reminding us that the journey towards a more ethical online world begins with mindful participation and a commitment to shaping technology for good.

CHAPTER 29: WHISPERS OF IDENTITY: THE ETHICS OF DIGITAL ANONYMITY

As our expedition through the diverse realms of the internet concludes, dear reader, we arrive at a crossroads where the mask meets the message, the whispers morph into roars, and the ethical quagmire of digital anonymity unfolds. Imagine not a bustling marketplace or a hidden forum, but a masquerade ball where identities dance in shadows, raising crucial questions about privacy, freedom, and the very nature of online interaction. In this complex arena, the whispers of anonymity morph into thunderous debates, leaving us to grapple with the ethical implications of a hidden presence in the digital world.

On one hand, anonymity empowers. Imagine the journalist exposing corruption without fear of reprisal, the activist advocating for a cause without facing persecution, or the individual seeking support for sensitive issues without judgment. For many, anonymity becomes a shield, protecting them from discrimination, harassment, and undue influence. It fosters open expression, empowers marginalized voices, and allows individuals to explore identities and opinions freely, pushing the boundaries of traditional discourse.

However, the cloak of anonymity can also harbour darkness. Imagine the cyberbully spewing hate speech with impunity, the troll disrupting online communities, or the criminal exploiting hidden spaces for nefarious activities. Anonymity can breed a sense of detachment from consequences, facilitating harmful behaviour and hindering accountability. The spread of misinformation, the erosion of trust online, and the potential for radicalization are all potential pitfalls, raising concerns about the ethical implications of this digital invisibility.

The debate becomes even more nuanced when considering the spectrum of anonymity. Imagine the difference between a pseudonym on a forum and complete anonymity achieved through complex encryption tools. The level of visibility, the ease of tracing, and the potential for harm all vary, demanding a multifaceted approach to navigating the ethical landscape. Moreover, cultural contexts play a crucial role, with varying attitudes towards anonymity across societies impacting online behaviours and perceptions.

Finding a balance between the benefits and risks of anonymity requires a comprehensive approach. Imagine robust content moderation practices combined with clear legal frameworks holding individuals accountable for their online actions, regardless of anonymity. Empowering users with digital literacy and promoting responsible online behaviour are crucial steps in fostering a healthy digital environment. Encouraging platforms to prioritize transparency and user privacy while acknowledging the limitations of complete anonymity also contributes to a more ethical approach.

As we move forward, we'll encounter stories of individuals and communities grappling with the complex realities of anonymity. We'll meet whistle-blowers using anonymity to expose wrongdoing, online communities fostering positive anonymity-backed interactions, and law enforcement agencies navigating the challenges of investigating crimes in encrypted spaces. Through their narratives, we'll gain a deeper understanding of the multifaceted nature of digital anonymity, the ethical considerations it presents, and the ongoing efforts to create a balanced future where anonymity protects without enabling harm.

So, dear reader, equip yourself with a discerning mind and a nuanced perspective. By engaging in open dialogue about the ethics of anonymity, advocating for responsible online practices, and supporting initiatives promoting digital citizenship, you can contribute to a future where anonymity serves as a tool for empowerment and positive change, ensuring that the online world remains a space for diverse voices, responsible expression, and ethical engagement, even in the shadows. Remember, even a single voice advocating for responsible anonymity can spark a ripple effect, reminding us that the true measure of our online presence lies not in visibility, but in the ethical values we choose to uphold, regardless of the mask we wear.

CHAPTER 30: WHISPERS OF HARMONY: FINDING THE BALANCE BETWEEN SECURITY, ANONYMITY, AND MORALITY

As our expedition through the internet's diverse landscapes culminates, dear reader, we arrive at a critical juncture where whispers of security, anonymity, and morality converge, demanding a harmonious resolution. Imagine not a bustling marketplace or a hidden forum, but a grand council chamber where the future of the digital world hangs in the balance. Here, the whispers morph into impassioned debates, echoing the struggle to reconcile individual rights with collective safety, privacy with accountability, and ethical principles with technological realities.

In this dynamic arena, competing values clash. Imagine citizens clamouring for robust security measures to combat online threats, while privacy advocates decry the erosion of anonymity and the chilling effect on free expression. Law enforcement seeks tools to investigate criminal activity, while tech companies grapple with balancing accessibility with data protection. Finding a harmonious equilibrium between these seemingly disparate needs lies at the heart of crafting a more ethical and sustainable digital future.

Striking this balance demands a multifaceted approach. Imagine robust cybersecurity measures implemented alongside user-centric privacy frameworks. Secure platforms and encryption technologies safeguard data without hindering legitimate activities. Clear legal frameworks and transparent law enforcement practices ensure accountability without trampling on digital rights. User education and digital literacy initiatives empower individuals to protect themselves online and navigate the complexities of data privacy.

The equation becomes even more intricate when considering the evolving landscape of technology. Imagine the rise of artificial intelligence, the proliferation of connected devices, and the increasing complexity of cyber threats. Adapting ethical frameworks and security measures to keep pace with this technological metamorphosis is crucial. Collaboration between diverse stakeholders – governments, tech companies, civil society organizations, and individuals – is essential to fostering an inclusive and responsible approach to these challenges.

However, navigating this ethical terrain requires more than just technological solutions. Imagine fostering a culture of responsible online behaviour. From ethical hacking practices to respectful online discourse, individual choices and actions play a pivotal role in shaping the moral fabric of the digital world. Cultivating compassion, empathy, and critical thinking are crucial tools in combating cyberbullying, misinformation, and online radicalization.

As we move forward, we'll encounter stories of individuals

and organizations striving to achieve this delicate balance. We'll meet cybersecurity experts building innovative defences, privacy advocates championing user rights, and digital rights activists challenging government overreach. Through their narratives, we'll gain a deeper understanding of the ongoing quest for a harmonious digital future, the challenges it faces, and the inspiring efforts to ensure that security, anonymity, and morality coexist in a mutually reinforcing way.

So, dear reader, arm yourself with a discerning mind and a commitment to collaborative action. By engaging in constructive dialogue about ethical technology development, advocating for responsible policies, and fostering a culture of digital citizenship, you can contribute to a future where security protects, anonymity empowers, and morality guides our interactions in the digital sphere. Remember, even a single voice advocating for balance can spark a ripple effect, reminding us that the responsibility for shaping a more ethical and harmonious online world lies not solely with tech giants or governments, but with each individual choosing to navigate the digital landscape with responsibility and respect.

PART VII: EDUCATION AND KNOWLEDGE

CHAPTER 31: DIGITAL LIBRARIES: ACCESS TO RESTRICTED INFORMATION

Our expedition through the vast landscapes of the internet concludes, dear reader, not with a hidden corner or a technological marvel, but with a treasure trove of knowledge: digital libraries. Imagine not a bustling marketplace or a dark forum, but a vast repository of information, some openly accessible, some restricted, all whispering tales of human endeavour and intellectual exploration. In this realm of knowledge, the whispers morph into the clinking of virtual pages, offering access to a wealth of information, raising questions about censorship, intellectual property, and the very nature of knowledge itself.

Within these digital walls, countless stories unfold. Imagine scholars accessing rare historical documents, students discovering obscure academic journals, and activists unearthing censored materials. Digital libraries offer a gateway to knowledge that transcends physical limitations, democratizing access to information that may have been previously out of reach for many. They can be havens for marginalized voices, repositories of cultural heritage, and invaluable tools for education and research.

Yet, navigating this realm of information demands a discerning mind. Imagine the ethical complexities surrounding copyrighted materials, government censorship, and the potential for misinformation. Striking a balance between open access and intellectual property rights, ensuring the accuracy and integrity of information, and safeguarding against the misuse of sensitive data are crucial challenges faced by these digital libraries.

The challenges extend beyond ethical considerations. Imagine the technical hurdles of digitizing vast collections, ensuring long-term preservation of digital data, and providing user-friendly interfaces for diverse audiences. The financial sustainability of these libraries, often reliant on grants or donations, also presents a significant obstacle.

Despite the challenges, the potential of digital libraries remains vast. Imagine educational platforms offering personalized learning experiences tailored to individual needs, historical archives fostering global understanding, and collaborative research initiatives tackling complex challenges. The applications seem boundless, promising to reshape education, research, and our access to knowledge itself.

As we move forward, we'll encounter stories of individuals and organizations pushing the boundaries of knowledge access. We'll meet librarians meticulously digitizing historical collections, activists creating digital libraries for censored materials, and educators utilizing these platforms to create innovative learning experiences. Through their narratives, we'll gain a deeper understanding of the transformative potential of digital libraries, the challenges they face, and the ongoing quest to create more equitable and open access to information for all.

So, dear reader, equip yourself with a critical mind and a sense of responsibility. By engaging in informed discussions about intellectual property rights, advocating for open access initiatives, and supporting organizations preserving our digital heritage, you can contribute to a future where knowledge flows freely, empowering individuals and communities to learn, explore, and create a more informed and just world. Remember, even a single click on a digital library website can unlock a universe of knowledge, reminding us that the boundaries of information are not set in stone and that the whispers of untold stories wait to be discovered in the vast digital libraries of our time.

CHAPTER 32: WHISPERS OF KNOWLEDGE: ONLINE COURSES AND UNDERGROUND ACADEMIA

Our expedition through the diverse landscapes of the internet concludes, dear reader, not with a bustling marketplace or a hidden forum, but with a classroom door creaking open in the vast digital realm. Imagine not just formal institutions, but a vibrant tapestry woven from independent creators, alternative communities, and self-directed learning journeys. In this realm of knowledge, whispers transform into the click of virtual pages and lectures, offering access to unconventional education and alternative perspectives, raising questions about accessibility, legitimacy, and the very definition of "academia."

Within this dynamic classroom, countless doors open to unique learning experiences. Imagine history buffs delving into forgotten narratives led by independent scholars, aspiring coders mastering new skills through online communities, and marginalized voices teaching courses on topics silenced by mainstream academia. Online courses and underground academia offer flexibility, affordability, and access to niche expertise often unavailable in traditional institutions. They can empower individuals, foster diverse perspectives, and challenge established narratives, democratizing knowledge, and creating inclusive learning spaces.

Yet, navigating this realm of learning demands a discerning mind. Imagine the challenges of verifying the quality and accuracy of information, identifying credible instructors, and avoiding misinformation or echo chambers. Evaluating content critically, seeking diverse perspectives, and engaging in informed discussions are crucial tools for navigating this diverse educational landscape.

The challenges extend beyond individual responsibility. Imagine concerns about plagiarism, copyright infringement, and the potential for the exploitation of learners in unregulated spaces. Robust ethical frameworks, transparent accreditation systems, and collaborative efforts between online platforms and learners are essential safeguards in upholding academic integrity and protecting individuals from harm.

Despite the challenges, the potential of online courses and underground academia remains vast. Imagine educational platforms tailored to individual learning styles, collaborative knowledge-sharing communities, and the integration of cutting-edge technologies into learning experiences. The applications seem boundless, promising to reshape education, democratize access to knowledge, and empower individuals to become lifelong learners.

As we move forward, we'll encounter stories of individuals and communities pushing the boundaries of traditional education. We'll meet independent creators developing innovative online courses, marginalized communities fostering alternative knowledge spaces, and learners actively shaping their educational journeys. Through their narratives, we'll gain a deeper understanding of the transformative potential of online courses and underground academia, the challenges they face, and the ongoing pursuit of a more inclusive and accessible educational landscape.

So, dear reader, equip yourself with a critical mind and a sense of curiosity. By engaging in informed discussions about educational quality and ethics, advocating for accessible learning opportunities, and supporting initiatives promoting responsible online education, you can contribute to a future where knowledge empowers all, regardless of background or circumstance. Remember, even a single online course completed or a forum discussion participated in can spark a journey of lifelong learning, reminding us that education is not confined to physical classrooms and that the whispers of knowledge can echo far and wide in the vast digital learning landscapes.

CHAPTER 33: WHISPERS OF COLLABORATION: COMMUNITIES OF ENTHUSIASTIC LEARNERS

As our expedition through the diverse realms of the internet draws to a close, dear reader, we arrive at a vibrant crossroads where whispers coalesce into the hum of collaborative learning. Imagine not a bustling marketplace or a hidden forum, but a campfire flickering within a vast digital campground, drawing together passionate individuals united by a thirst for knowledge. In this dynamic space, whispers transform into shared ideas, fuelled by curiosity, collaboration, and the boundless potential of shared learning.

Within this virtual campfire circle, countless stories unfold. Imagine amateur astronomers deciphering celestial mysteries through online forums, hobbyist coders honing their skills in collaborative programming challenges, and history buffs piecing together forgotten narratives in digital communities. These communities of enthusiastic learners transcend geographical boundaries, fostering connections, encouraging support, and offering an unparalleled platform for collective knowledge exploration.

Yet, navigating this collaborative landscape demands a discerning mind. Imagine the challenges of verifying information, identifying reliable sources, and navigating potential biases within echo chambers. Critical thinking, open-mindedness, and the ability to engage in respectful dialogue are crucial tools for harnessing the full potential of these learning communities.

The challenges extend beyond individual responsibility. Imagine concerns about misinformation, online harassment, and the potential for echo chambers reinforcing harmful stereotypes. Robust moderation practices, clear community guidelines, and fostering an inclusive environment are crucial safeguards in ensuring these spaces promote healthy learning and respectful interactions.

Despite the challenges, the potential of communities of enthusiastic learners remains vast. Imagine collaborative research projects tackling complex challenges, peer-to-peer mentoring fostering skill development, and the collective exploration of emerging technologies enriching individual understanding. The applications seem boundless, promising to reshape learning, empower individuals, and create vibrant spaces for lifelong knowledge acquisition.

As we move forward, we'll encounter stories of individuals and communities pushing the boundaries of collaborative learning. We'll meet online communities tackling global challenges, passionate individuals spearheading citizen science initiatives, and platforms fostering peer-to-peer mentoring and knowledge exchange. Through their narratives, we'll gain a deeper understanding of the transformative potential of these communities, the challenges they face, and the ongoing quest to create a more inclusive and collaborative learning landscape for all.

So, dear reader, equip yourself with a collaborative spirit and a thirst for knowledge. By actively participating in discussions, sharing your expertise, and fostering respectful dialogue, you can contribute to a future where learning transcends physical boundaries, communities empower individuals, and collaboration fuels the collective pursuit of knowledge. Remember, even a single shared resource or insightful comment can spark a chain reaction of learning, reminding us that the potential for collective knowledge exploration lies within each of us, and the whispers of shared understanding can ignite a brighter future for learning in the digital sphere.

CHAPTER 34: WHISPERS IN THE SHADOWS: NAVIGATING CENSORED INFORMATION IN RESTRICTED AREAS

Our expedition through the sprawling landscapes of the internet concludes, dear reader, not with a bustling marketplace or a hidden forum, but at a crossroads guarded by digital barriers. Imagine not just websites and apps, but entire regions shrouded in secrecy, where information itself becomes a battleground. In this realm, whispers transform into hushed conversations, carrying stories of censored knowledge, political dissent, and the ongoing struggle for access to truth. Here, we tread carefully, grappling with the complex questions of freedom of information, cultural values, and the ethical boundaries of navigating restricted areas.

Within these digital borders, narratives unfold under the veil of censorship. Imagine journalists risking their lives to expose human rights abuses, activists utilizing encrypted channels to organize for change, and artists expressing their dissent through subversive online platforms. In restricted areas, information becomes a weapon, and accessing it can be an act of courage, defying authority and risking personal safety. Yet, the thirst for knowledge persists, reminding us that information empowers, connects, and fuels the fight for justice.

But navigating this landscape demands a discerning mind and a nuanced perspective. Imagine the challenges of verifying information amidst propaganda and misinformation, balancing individual rights with national security concerns, and avoiding inadvertently harming those seeking our support. Critical thinking, cultural sensitivity, and responsible information handling are crucial tools for engaging with censored information ethically.

The challenges extend beyond individual responsibility. Imagine governments wielding powerful tools to block websites, monitor online activity, and silence dissenting voices. Balancing national security with freedom of expression, fostering transparency and accountability within governments, and advocating for international collaboration are crucial steps towards creating a more open and equitable online environment.

Despite the challenges, the fight for access to information in restricted areas remains undeterred. Imagine innovative technologies circumventing censorship, global solidarity movements amplifying marginalized voices, and individuals courageously speaking truth to power. The applications of open access and responsible information sharing seem boundless, promising to empower citizens, hold authorities accountable, and foster a more just and informed global community.

As we move forward, we'll encounter stories of individuals and organizations leading the charge against censorship. We'll meet journalists risking their lives to report from conflict zones, tech developers creating circumvention tools, and human rights activists working tirelessly to expose injustices. Through their narratives, we'll gain a deeper understanding of the complexities of information access in restricted areas, the ongoing fight for freedom of expression, and the inspiring efforts to ensure that knowledge becomes a tool for empowerment, not oppression.

So, dear reader, equip yourself with a critical mind and a commitment to truth. By engaging in informed discussions about online censorship, supporting organizations advocating for transparency, and responsibly sharing information, you can contribute to a future where knowledge transcends borders, empowers individuals, and illuminates the path towards a more just and equitable world. Remember, even a single voice raised in support of open access can resonate far and wide, reminding us that the fight for information freedom is not confined to distant lands, but a responsibility shared by all who value truth and the right to know.

CHAPTER 35: CODING CONSTELLATIONS: THE RISE OF PROGRAMMING AND TECH SKILLS PLATFORMS

Our expedition through the vast digital realm concludes, dear reader, not with a bustling marketplace or a hidden forum, but with a vibrant nebula of learning communities. Imagine galaxies of online platforms, each a constellation of coding challenges, project tutorials, and passionate learners, all united by a shared mission: mastering tech skills. In this dynamic sphere, whispers transform into the clatter of virtual keyboards, as individuals embark on journeys of self-improvement, fuelled by the limitless potential of tech knowledge.

Within these digital constellations, countless stories unfold. Imagine aspiring developers honing their skills through interactive challenges, aspiring data scientists delving into complex algorithms, and freelance designers collaborating on cutting-edge projects. These platforms democratize tech education, removing geographical barriers, catering to diverse learning styles, and empowering individuals to transform their lives through code.

Yet, navigating this learning landscape demands a discerning mind. Imagine the challenges of identifying credible resources, avoiding misinformation, and finding a platform that aligns with your learning goals. Critical thinking, self-motivation, and the ability to filter information effectively are crucial tools for maximizing your learning experience.

The challenges extend beyond individual responsibility. Imagine concerns about plagiarism, copyright infringement, and the potential for predatory practices within certain platforms. Robust moderation practices, transparent user agreements, and collaborative efforts between platforms and learners are essential safeguards in ensuring a safe and ethical learning environment.

Despite the challenges, the potential of programming and tech skills platforms remains vast. Imagine personalized learning pathways tailored to individual needs, cutting-edge instructional methods utilizing AR/VR technology, and global communities fostering peer-to-peer learning and support. The applications seem boundless, promising to reshape education, democratize access to tech expertise, and empower individuals to become active participants in the digital future.

As we move forward, we'll encounter stories of individuals and communities pushing the boundaries of tech skills development. We'll meet self-taught coders landing dream jobs, online communities tackling global challenges through collaborative coding projects, and platforms pioneering innovative AI-powered learning experiences. Through their narratives, we'll gain a deeper understanding of the transformative potential of these platforms, the challenges they face, and the ongoing quest to create a more inclusive and accessible tech education landscape.

So, dear reader, equip yourself with a curious mind and a thirst for knowledge. By actively engaging in learning challenges, sharing your expertise with others, and advocating for ethical and responsible platform practices, you can contribute to a future where tech skills empower all, regardless of background or circumstance. Remember, even a single line of code written or a tutorial completed can spark a journey of innovation, reminding us that the potential for self-improvement and collective progress lies within each of us, fuelled by the vibrant constellations of knowledge available in the digital learning sphere.

PART VIII: HEALTH AND WELLNESS

CHAPTER 36: ACCESS TO RESTRICTED MEDICATION

In the vast, uncharted territories of the digital age, the dark web often emerges as a realm shrouded in mystery and maligned by its association with illicit activities. Yet, within this digital underworld, there lies an unexpected beacon of hope for many: the provision of restricted medication to those in dire need. This chapter embarks on an expedition into the complexities of accessing medication through the dark web, illuminating the ethical, legal, and health landscapes navigated by those who venture into its depths.

The dark web, accessible only through specialized software that anonymizes user identities and locations, hosts a myriad of services and goods, some legal, others less so. Among these are pharmacies operating in the shadows, providing access to medications that are either heavily restricted or exorbitantly priced in conventional markets. For individuals suffering from chronic pain, rare diseases, or life-threatening conditions, these clandestine dispensaries offer a lifeline—an alternative route to the medicines they desperately require.

One such story is that of Maria, a pseudonym for a woman battling a rare form of cancer. Traditional healthcare channels had ensnared her in a labyrinth of paperwork, denied insurance claims, and insurmountable costs for medication. Driven to desperation, Maria turned to the dark web. There, she found a vendor who supplied her with the necessary medication at a fraction of the price. "It was either watch my life slip away or take a risk," Maria recounts. "I chose to fight for my life."

The ethical conundrum presented by Maria's story is emblematic of the broader debate surrounding dark web pharmacies. On one hand, these platforms can circumvent legal frameworks and safety regulations, posing significant risks to public health. Counterfeit or improperly handled medications can lead to adverse effects, further complicating patients' conditions. On the other hand, they represent a critical lifeline for those marginalized by the traditional healthcare system.

Legal scholars and ethicists argue that the existence of such markets underscores systemic failures in global healthcare systems—failures that drive individuals to seek remedies in the digital underworld. "The dark web, in this context, becomes a mirror reflecting the inequities and inefficiencies of our healthcare institutions," notes Dr. Elena Vasquez, a leading researcher on health policy.

The journey into the dark web's pharmacies is fraught with danger, not just from law enforcement but from the threat of exploitation by unscrupulous vendors. Yet, for many, the potential benefits outweigh the risks. The decision to venture into this realm is often driven by a sense of desperation and a lack of viable alternatives.

Navigating the dark web requires not just technical acumen but a keen sense of vigilance. Prospective buyers must wade through a morass of vendor reviews, seeking out those with a reputation for reliability and quality. Transactions are conducted in cryptocurrencies, adding layers of complexity and risk to the already perilous endeavour.

Despite the dangers, the demand for dark web pharmacies continues to grow, driven by the global disparities in healthcare access. In countries with stringent drug laws or under-resourced healthcare systems, these platforms can offer a vital, albeit risky, source of necessary medication.

This chapter concludes with a call to action, urging policymakers, healthcare providers, and society at large to confront the underlying issues that drive individuals to such extremes. "The dark web's pharmacies are a symptom of a larger disease," Dr. Vasquez asserts. "Until we address the root causes—until we build a more equitable, accessible, and compassionate healthcare system—these digital lifelines will remain indispensable for the marginalized."

In the final analysis, "Access to Restricted Medication" presents a nuanced exploration of the dark web's role in circumventing healthcare barriers. It challenges readers to consider the moral implications of a world where life-saving medication is just a clandestine click away, and it highlights the urgent need for systemic reform. Through the lens of the dark web, we gain insight into the depths of human resilience and the lengths to which individuals will go to preserve their health and dignity in the face of systemic adversity.

CHAPTER 37: WHISPERS OF HOPE: MENTAL HEALTH PLATFORMS AND SUPPORT ON THE DARK WEB

Our expedition through the vast digital landscapes concludes, dear reader, not with a bustling marketplace or a hidden forum, but in a sanctuary bathed in empathy and understanding. Imagine not just websites and apps, but a haven for individuals navigating the complexities of mental well-being. In this realm of support, whispers transform into shared experiences, where anonymity meets acceptance, and technology empowers individuals seeking connection and healing. As we step into this sensitive sphere, we tread carefully, acknowledging the inherent challenges and ethical considerations surrounding mental health in the digital world.

Within these safe harbour platforms, countless stories unfold. Imagine individuals battling anxiety finding solace in anonymous support groups, survivors of trauma connecting with others who understand their struggles, and those questioning their identities discovering supportive communities. In this digital sanctuary, anonymity can foster vulnerability, enabling individuals to express themselves freely without fear of judgment, igniting a sense of belonging and fostering peer support.

Yet, navigating this landscape of support demands a discerning mind and a critical eye. Imagine the challenges of identifying reliable resources, recognizing potential misinformation or harmful advice, and safeguarding against exploitation within vulnerable communities. Critical thinking, self-awareness, and the ability to identify trustworthy resources are crucial tools for navigating these platforms responsibly.

The challenges extend beyond individual responsibility. Imagine concerns about potential manipulation, predatory behaviour, and the spread of misinformation within certain platforms. Robust moderation practices, clear community guidelines, and collaborations between platforms and mental health professionals are essential safeguards in ensuring a safe and supportive environment.

Despite the challenges, the potential of mental health platforms on the dark web remains significant. Imagine self-management tools tailored to individual needs, peer-to-peer support networks offering encouragement and validation, and access to expert guidance when needed. The applications seem boundless, promising to improve access to mental health resources, foster understanding, and acceptance, and empower individuals to reclaim their well-being.

As we move forward, we'll encounter stories of individuals and organizations pushing the boundaries of mental health support in the digital world. We'll meet peer support networks providing crucial connections, tech developers creating innovative tools for self-management, and ethical platforms prioritizing safety and well-being. Through their narratives, we'll gain a deeper understanding of the transformative potential of these platforms, the challenges they face, and the ongoing quest to create a more inclusive and supportive online environment for mental health.

So, dear reader, equip yourself with a compassionate heart and a commitment to safety. By engaging in respectful discussions about mental health awareness, advocating for responsible platform practices, and promoting resources that prioritize well-being, you can contribute to a future where technology empowers individuals to reclaim their mental health, fostering a sense of connection and support in the vast digital landscape. Remember, even a single message of encouragement or a shared experience can ignite hope and illuminate a path towards healing, reminding us that the whispers of support in the digital world can bloom into a chorus of empowerment and collective well-being.

CHAPTER 38: WHISPERS OF WELLNESS: EXPLORING UNCONVENTIONAL THERAPIES AND REMEDIES ON THE DARK WEB

Our expedition through the intricate labyrinths of the internet concludes not with a bustling marketplace or a hidden forum but with a whispered conversation about unconventional paths to wellness. Imagine not just websites and apps, but a tapestry woven from ancient wisdom, alternative healing practices, and personal journeys towards well-being. In this realm of exploration, whispers transform into shared experiences, where curiosity intertwines with caution, and individuals seek solutions beyond mainstream medicine. As we step into this sensitive space, we tread carefully, acknowledging the inherent complexities and ethical considerations surrounding unconventional therapies in the digital realm.

Within these diverse forums and communities, countless narratives unfold. Imagine individuals battling chronic illnesses finding solace in holistic remedies shared by others, those seeking emotional healing discovering alternative therapeutic approaches, and individuals questioning conventional narratives connecting with communities exploring self-healing practices. While these platforms offer a space for exploration and support, the lack of regulation and potential for misinformation necessitate a discerning approach.

Navigating this landscape demands a critical mind and a healthy dose of scepticism. Imagine the challenges of differentiating credible information from anecdotal experiences, identifying potential risks associated with untested remedies, and avoiding harmful practices disguised as alternative therapies. Critical thinking, thorough research, and consulting qualified healthcare professionals are crucial tools for responsible engagement with these platforms.

The challenges extend beyond individual responsibility. Imagine concerns about misinformation, predatory practices, and the exploitation of vulnerable individuals seeking solace. Robust moderation practices, clear community guidelines, and collaborations between platforms and healthcare professionals are essential safeguards in ensuring a safe and responsible space for exploration.

Despite the challenges, the potential for responsible exploration of unconventional therapies remains significant. Imagine access to diverse healing practices based on traditional wisdom, platforms fostering open dialogue and knowledge sharing, and empowering individuals to take charge of their well-being through informed choices. The applications seem boundless, promising to expand our understanding of health and wellness, fostering respect for diverse approaches, and empowering individuals to seek complementary solutions alongside conventional medicine.

As we move forward, we'll encounter stories of individuals and communities pushing the boundaries of wellness through unconventional means. We'll meet individuals finding healing through ancient practices like yoga and meditation, communities exploring the potential of plant-based remedies, and platforms promoting responsible and informed exploration of alternative therapies. Through their narratives, we'll gain a deeper understanding of the transformative potential of these approaches, the challenges they face, and the ongoing quest to create a more inclusive and empowering space for diverse paths to well-being.

So, dear reader, equip yourself with a curious mind and a commitment to informed exploration. By engaging in respectful discussions about alternative therapies, advocating for responsible platform practices, and promoting evidence-based information, you can contribute to a future where individuals have access to diverse well-being resources, navigate online platforms responsibly, and make informed choices on their journey towards holistic health. Remember, even a single shared experience or insightful resource can spark a journey of self-discovery and empower individuals to explore the whispers of unconventional wellness within themselves and the vast digital landscape.

CHAPTER 39: WHISPERS OF SUPPORT: NAVIGATING HEALTH FORUMS AND PATIENT COMMUNITIES ON THE DARK WEB

Our expedition through the diverse landscapes of the internet concludes not with a bustling marketplace or a hidden forum but with a campfire flickering within a virtual support circle. Imagine not just websites and chats, but a space where whispers transform into shared experiences, fostering connection and understanding among individuals navigating similar health challenges. In this realm of patient communities, where anonymity meets empathy, we tread carefully, acknowledging the inherent complexities and ethical considerations surrounding health information on the dark web.

Within these vibrant forums and communities, countless

narratives unfold. Imagine individuals battling chronic illnesses finding solace in shared experiences, patients facing rare conditions discovering valuable information, and those on unique treatment paths connecting with others who understand their journeys. These platforms offer a space for peer support, emotional validation, and information exchange, potentially empowering individuals to feel less alone and find strength in the community.

Yet, navigating this landscape demands a discerning mind and a critical eye. Imagine the challenges of verifying information accuracy, recognizing potential misinformation or harmful advice, and avoiding exploitation within vulnerable communities. Critical thinking, self-awareness, and the ability to identify credible sources are crucial tools for responsible engagement with these platforms.

The challenges extend beyond individual responsibility. Imagine concerns about misinformation, predatory practices, and the exploitation of vulnerable individuals seeking support. Robust moderation practices, clear community guidelines, and collaborations between platforms and healthcare professionals are essential safeguards in ensuring a safe and supportive environment.

Despite the challenges, the potential of health forums and patient communities on the dark web remains significant. Imagine access to diverse perspectives and lived experiences, platforms fostering respectful discussions and knowledge sharing, and empowering individuals to advocate for their health needs. The applications seem boundless, promising to offer support beyond geographical limitations, foster understanding of unique health journeys, and empower individuals to navigate the healthcare system with more confidence.

As we move forward, we'll encounter stories of individuals

and communities pushing the boundaries of patient support and empowerment. We'll meet individuals finding strength in anonymous online communities, patient advocates utilizing platforms to raise awareness, and tech developers creating innovative tools to connect patients with reliable information. Through their narratives, we'll gain a deeper understanding of the transformative potential of these platforms, the challenges they face, and the ongoing quest to create a more inclusive and supportive online environment for individuals facing health challenges.

So, dear reader, equip yourself with a compassionate heart and a commitment to responsible engagement. By actively participating in respectful discussions, promoting trustworthy information sources, and advocating for platform accountability, you can contribute to a future where technology empowers individuals to find support, navigate their health journeys with confidence, and contribute to a collective understanding of diverse health experiences. Remember, even a single shared experience or insightful comment can spark hope and support, reminding us that the whispers of shared voices in the digital world can ignite a chorus of empowerment and collective well-being.

CHAPTER 40:
WHISPERS OF HOPE: UNRAVELLING THE SECRETS OF RARE DISEASES ON THE DARK WEB

Our digital odyssey draws to a close, dear reader, not with a bustling marketplace or hidden forum, but with a flickering candle illuminating a path towards understanding. Imagine not just websites and databases, but a community dedicated to unearthing the secrets of rare diseases, where whispers transform into shared experiences, and anonymity fuels collaboration in the fight against the unknown. In this realm of hope and resilience, we tread carefully, acknowledging the inherent complexities and ethical considerations surrounding sensitive medical information on the dark web.

Within these vibrant forums and communities, countless narratives unfold. Imagine individuals battling rare conditions finding solace in shared experiences, families seeking answers connecting with researchers breaking new ground, and patients embarking on clinical trials discovering invaluable information beyond mainstream sources. These platforms offer a space for peer support, information exchange, and even collaborative research, potentially fostering hope, and empowering individuals to play an active role in their healthcare journeys.

Yet, navigating this landscape demands a discerning mind and a critical eye. Imagine the challenges of verifying information accuracy, identifying potential misinformation or harmful advice, and protecting the privacy of vulnerable individuals. Critical thinking, self-awareness, and the ability to identify credible sources are crucial tools for responsible engagement with these platforms.

The challenges extend beyond individual responsibility. Imagine concerns about exploitation, predatory practices, and the spread of misinformation within unregulated platforms. Robust moderation practices, clear community guidelines, and collaborations between platforms, patient advocacy groups, and medical professionals are essential safeguards in ensuring a safe and reliable environment for information exchange.

Despite the challenges, the potential of information sharing on the dark web for rare diseases remains significant. Imagine access to diverse perspectives and lived experiences, platforms fostering open communication and collaborative research, and empowering individuals to advocate for their needs and contribute to scientific progress. The applications seem boundless, promising to accelerate research efforts, foster international collaboration, and ultimately offer hope and potential breakthroughs for individuals grappling with rare conditions.

As we move forward, we'll encounter stories of individuals and communities pushing the boundaries of information access and research. We'll meet patients utilizing online platforms to connect with researchers, advocacy groups leveraging the dark web to raise awareness, and tech developers creating innovative tools to facilitate data sharing and analysis. Through their narratives, we'll gain a deeper understanding of the transformative potential of these platforms, the challenges they face, and the ongoing quest to create a more inclusive and collaborative environment for rare disease communities.

So, dear reader, equip yourself with a compassionate heart and a commitment to responsible exploration. By actively participating in respectful discussions, promoting trustworthy information sources, and advocating for platform accountability, you can contribute to a future where technology empowers individuals to find support, contribute to research efforts, and advocate for equitable access to healthcare for all. Remember, even a single shared experience or insightful comment can spark hope and collaboration, reminding us that the whispers of shared voices in the digital world can become a chorus of hope and progress in the fight against rare diseases.

PART IX:
ENTERTAINMENT

CHAPTER 41: WHISPERS ON THE SILVER SCREEN: EXPLORING INDIE FILMS AND DOCUMENTARIES ON THE DARK WEB

Our digital odyssey concludes, dear reader, not with a bustling marketplace or a hidden forum, but in a shadowy cinema where independent voices flicker to life. Imagine not just mainstream releases, but a tapestry woven from raw narratives, bold documentaries, and unconventional visions. Here, independent stories find their audience, whispers transform into captivating narratives, and the dark web offers a platform for voices otherwise silenced. As we step into this realm of artistic expression, we tread carefully, acknowledging the legal and ethical considerations surrounding copyrighted content.

Within these virtual screening rooms, countless stories unfold. Imagine filmmakers defying censorship to expose injustices, documentarians shedding light on untold truths, and aspiring creators finding a platform for their unique perspectives. In this sanctuary for independent artistry, the dark web provides an escape from commercial constraints, fostering experimentation and diverse storytelling.

Yet, navigating this landscape demands a discerning mind and a critical eye. Imagine the challenges of verifying the legitimacy of content, avoiding copyright infringement, and ensuring the ethical representation of sensitive topics. Responsible consumption habits, respect for intellectual property rights, and awareness of potentially harmful content are crucial for engaging with these platforms ethically.

The challenges extend beyond individual responsibility. Imagine concerns about piracy, unauthorized distribution, and the potential for exploitation of content creators. Robust content-sharing agreements, clear community guidelines, and collaborations between platforms and filmmakers are essential safeguards in promoting ethical and sustainable artistic expression.

Despite the challenges, the potential for independent artistic expression in the dark web remains significant. Imagine access to diverse narratives and filmmaking styles, platforms fostering open dialogue and critical analysis, and empowering creators to reach audiences beyond geographical limitations. The applications seem boundless, promising to enrich cultural landscapes, promote diverse perspectives, and empower aspiring filmmakers to connect with their audiences directly.

As we move forward, we'll encounter stories of individuals and communities pushing the boundaries of independent filmmaking. We'll meet documentarians utilizing the dark web to bypass censorship, filmmakers finding innovative ways to distribute their work ethically, and platforms dedicated to promoting independent artistry responsibly. Through their narratives, we'll gain a deeper understanding of the transformative potential of these platforms, the challenges they face, and the ongoing quest to create a more inclusive and accessible space for independent voices.

So, dear reader, equip yourself with a curious mind and a commitment to responsible engagement. By actively supporting ethical distribution platforms, promoting critical discussions about intellectual property rights, and advocating for fair compensation for creators, you can contribute to a future where technology empowers independent voices, fosters cultural diversity, and ensures responsible access to artistic expression on the dark web. Remember, even a single shared film or insightful review can spark dialogue and appreciation, reminding us that the whispers of independent stories in the digital world can ignite a vibrant tapestry of cultural expression and artistic freedom.

Please note: While this chapter explores the potential of the dark web for independent films and documentaries, it is crucial to prioritize ethical considerations and avoid engaging in piracy or copyright infringement. Supporting creators through official channels and advocating for fair access to independent art remain ethical and impactful ways to contribute to the cultural landscape.

CHAPTER 42: WHISPERS OF MELODY: UNCONVENTIONAL MUSIC AND THE DARK WEB

Our digital expedition draws to a close, dear reader, not with a bustling marketplace or a hidden forum, but with a concert hall buzzing with unconventional sounds. Imagine not just mainstream hits, but a symphony woven from experimental compositions, raw talent, and voices seeking expression beyond the confines of industry norms. In this realm of sonic exploration, whispers of melody transform into captivating compositions, and anonymity fuels artistic freedom. As we step into this vibrant soundscape, we tread carefully, acknowledging the legal and ethical considerations surrounding copyrighted content.

Within these virtual stages, countless stories unfold. Imagine musicians defying limitations to share their unique styles, independent artists finding a global audience, and marginalized voices rising through the digital noise. This sanctuary for unconventional music offers a platform for experimentation, fostering diverse genres and breaking free from commercial pressures.

Yet, navigating this landscape demands a discerning ear and a critical mind. Imagine the challenges of verifying the legitimacy of content, avoiding copyright infringement, and ensuring fair compensation for artists. Responsible consumption habits, respect for intellectual property rights, and awareness of potentially harmful content are crucial for engaging with these platforms ethically.

The challenges extend beyond individual responsibility. Imagine concerns about piracy, unauthorized distribution, and the potential for exploitation of artists within unregulated platforms. Robust content-sharing agreements, clear community guidelines, and collaborations between platforms and musicians are essential safeguards in promoting ethical and sustainable artistic expression.

Despite the challenges, the potential for unconventional music on the dark web remains significant. Imagine access to diverse genres and artistic explorations, platforms fostering open dialogue and critical discourse, and empowering musicians to connect with audiences beyond geographical limitations. The applications seem boundless, promising to enrich cultural landscapes, promote independent voices, and empower aspiring artists to share their creative visions.

As we move forward, we'll encounter stories of individuals and communities pushing the boundaries of musical expression. We'll meet musicians utilizing the dark web to bypass censorship, artists finding innovative ways to distribute their work ethically, and platforms dedicated to promoting unconventional music responsibly. Through their narratives, we'll gain a deeper understanding of the transformative potential of these platforms, the challenges they face, and the ongoing quest to create a more inclusive and accessible space for independent voices.

So, dear reader, equip yourself with a curious ear and a commitment to responsible engagement. By actively supporting ethical distribution platforms, promoting critical discussions about intellectual property rights, and advocating for fair compensation for artists, you can contribute to a future where technology empowers unconventional music, fosters cultural diversity, and ensures responsible access to artistic expression. Remember, even a single shared song or insightful review can spark discovery and appreciation, reminding us that the whispers of unheard melodies in the digital world can ignite a symphony of creativity and artistic freedom.

Please note: While this chapter explores the potential of the dark web for unconventional music, it is crucial to prioritize ethical considerations and avoid engaging in piracy or copyright infringement. Supporting artists through official channels and advocating for fair access to independent art remain ethical and impactful ways to contribute to the cultural landscape.

CHAPTER 43: PIXELS OF NOSTALGIA: RETRO GAMING AND MODS ON THE DARK WEB

Our digital escapade concludes, dear reader, not with a bustling marketplace or a hidden forum, but in a pixelated world where classic games flicker back to life. Imagine not just AAA releases, but a treasure trove of retro titles and fan-made modifications, where whispers of nostalgia transform into nostalgic adventures and the dark web offers a sanctuary for gamers yearning for simpler times. As we step into this realm of rekindled memories, we tread carefully, acknowledging the legal and ethical considerations surrounding copyright and intellectual property.

Within these virtual arcades, countless stories unfold. Imagine seasoned gamers rediscovering childhood favourites, aspiring developers learning through mudding communities, and marginalized communities finding solace in shared gaming experiences. This haven for retro gaming offers a platform for preserving digital history, fostering creativity through mods, and connecting individuals across generations with a shared passion for classic titles.

Yet, navigating this landscape demands a discerning mind and a responsible approach. Imagine the challenges of verifying the legitimacy of ROMs and mods, avoiding copyright infringement, and ensuring the safety and security of downloaded content. Responsible practices, respect for intellectual property rights, and awareness of potential malware are crucial for engaging with these platforms ethically.

The challenges extend beyond individual responsibility. Imagine concerns about piracy, unauthorized distribution, and the exploitation of developers within unregulated platforms. Robust content-sharing agreements, clear community guidelines, and collaborations between platforms and copyright holders are essential safeguards in promoting ethical and sustainable access to retro games and mods.

Despite the challenges, the potential for retro gaming and modding on the dark web remains significant. Imagine access to a vast library of preserved titles, and platforms fostering open dialogue and collaborative modding, and empowering individuals to customize their gaming experiences beyond commercial limitations. The applications seem boundless, promising to enrich gaming history, promote creative expression, and offer unique experiences for nostalgic gamers and aspiring developers alike.

As we move forward, we'll encounter stories of individuals and communities pushing the boundaries of retro gaming and modding. We'll meet gamers utilizing the dark web to access rare titles ethically, modders creating innovative experiences for classic games, and platforms dedicated to responsible preservation and community-driven modding. Through their narratives, we'll gain a deeper understanding of the transformative potential of these platforms, the challenges they face, and the ongoing quest to create a more inclusive and accessible space for retro gaming enthusiasts.

So, dear reader, equip yourself with a nostalgic heart and a commitment to responsible engagement. By actively supporting ethical distribution platforms, promoting awareness of copyright laws, and advocating for fair compensation for developers, you can contribute to a future where technology empowers retro gaming and modding, fosters cultural preservation and creative expression, and ensures responsible access to digital gaming legacies. Remember, even a single shared ROM or insightful mod review can spark joy and rekindle forgotten memories, reminding us that the whispers of classic game worlds in the digital sphere can ignite a vibrant community of nostalgic players and passionate creators.

Please note: While this chapter explores the potential of the dark web for retro gaming and modding, it is crucial to prioritize ethical considerations and avoid engaging in piracy or copyright infringement. Supporting official releases, utilizing legal alternatives, and respecting intellectual property rights remain ethical and impactful ways to contribute to the gaming community and preserve digital history.

CHAPTER 44: WHISPERS OF DISSENT: UNCENSORED VOICES AND FORBIDDEN NARRATIVES ON THE DARK WEB

Our digital expedition concludes not with a bustling marketplace or a hidden forum, but in a clandestine library where banned books whisper forbidden tales. Imagine not just mainstream publications, but a haven for censored voices, dissident writers, and narratives challenging oppressive regimes. In this realm of forbidden knowledge, whispers transform into powerful stories, anonymity fuels fearless expression, and the dark web offers a sanctuary for voices otherwise silenced. As we step into this sensitive space, we tread carefully, acknowledging the ethical and legal complexities surrounding copyrighted material and potentially controversial content.

Within these hushed shelves, countless stories unfold. Imagine writers defying censorship to expose human rights abuses, journalists risking their lives to report on forbidden truths, and marginalized communities finding a platform to share their narratives without fear of reprisal. This sanctuary for uncensored literature offers a space for free expression, challenging dominant narratives, and fostering a global understanding of diverse perspectives.

Yet, navigating this landscape demands a discerning mind and a critical eye. Imagine the challenges of verifying the legitimacy of content, distinguishing factual reporting from propaganda, and ensuring responsible engagement with potentially sensitive topics. Critical thinking, source verification, and awareness of personal safety considerations are crucial for exploring these platforms ethically.

The challenges extend beyond individual responsibility. Imagine concerns about government surveillance, infiltration by malicious actors, and the exploitation of vulnerable individuals within unregulated platforms. Robust security measures, clear community guidelines, and collaborations between platforms, writers, and human rights organizations are essential safeguards in ensuring a safe and responsible space for uncensored expression.

Despite the challenges, the potential for uncensored literature on the dark web remains significant. Imagine access to diverse narratives and critical perspectives often suppressed by oppressive regimes, platforms fostering open dialogue and critical analysis, and empowering writers to reach audiences beyond geographical limitations. The applications seem boundless, promising to promote transparency and accountability, foster global understanding, and empower individuals to advocate for freedom of expression worldwide.

As we move forward, we'll encounter stories of writers and communities pushing the boundaries of free expression. We'll meet journalists utilizing the dark web to bypass censorship, writers finding innovative ways to distribute their work securely, and platforms dedicated to promoting uncensored literature responsibly. Through their narratives, we'll gain a deeper understanding of the transformative potential of these platforms, the challenges they face, and the ongoing quest to create a more inclusive and accessible space for silenced voices.

So, dear reader, equip yourself with a curious mind and a commitment to responsible engagement. By actively supporting organizations promoting freedom of expression, advocating for safe and secure platforms, and promoting critical thinking skills, you can contribute to a future where technology empowers uncensored voices, challenges injustices, and ensures responsible access to diverse narratives worldwide. Remember, even a single shared story or insightful review can spark dialogue and awareness, reminding us that the whispers of banned books in the digital world can ignite a chorus of dissent and a global movement for freedom of expression.

Please note: While this chapter explores the potential of the dark web for uncensored literature, it is crucial to prioritize ethical considerations and legal boundaries. Engaging with copyrighted material responsibly, verifying information sources critically, and prioritizing your safety within potentially sensitive online spaces remain paramount. Supporting organizations advocating for freedom of expression and responsible access to information through legal channels are impactful ways to contribute to a more informed and just world.

CHAPTER 45: UNOFFICIAL FAN CONTENT AND CREATIONS - WHERE PASSION MEETS COPYRIGHT

As we delve deeper into the vibrant yet shadowy corners of the dark web, we encounter a surprising phenomenon: a thriving community dedicated to unofficial fan content and creations. Imagine a hidden bazaar, its stalls not brimming with tangible goods, but with whispered odes to beloved characters, reimagined storylines, and artistic expressions inspired by established franchises.

On the surface, this realm might seem like a haven for copyright infringement. However, upon closer examination, a more nuanced picture emerges. While blatant piracy and disregard for intellectual property certainly exist, many creators operate within a complex grey area, driven by passion, artistic expression, and a desire to engage with beloved narratives in ways not offered by official channels.

Let us begin by acknowledging the ethical concerns.

Distributing copyrighted material without permission can have significant financial and legal ramifications for both creators and consumers. Moreover, unauthorized adaptations can sometimes misrepresent or disrespect the original works and their creators.

However, the story doesn't end there. Many fan communities on the dark web operate with respect and admiration for the source material. They create non-profit fan fiction, artwork, and even games, often pushing creative boundaries and exploring thematic depths not ventured into by official channels. These creations breathe new life into established narratives, fostering deeper engagement and community among fans.

Furthermore, the anonymity offered by the dark web empowers marginalized voices and allows creators to explore controversial themes or engage in critical interpretations that might face resistance or censorship on mainstream platforms. This opens up avenues for diverse perspectives and enriches the overall creative landscape.

But navigating this realm requires caution and ethical considerations. Responsible engagement involves seeking permission from copyright holders whenever possible, clearly crediting original creators, and avoiding blatant plagiarism or commercial exploitation of fan works. Additionally, respecting the original work's integrity and avoiding harmful misinterpretations remains crucial.

One fascinating aspect of this hidden fandom is the emergence of collaborative projects. Fan communities on the dark web come together to create intricate narratives, elaborate game mods, and even online role-playing experiences, fostering a sense of belonging and shared creativity. This collaborative spirit pushes the boundaries of traditional fan engagement and showcases the power of collective imagination.

However, challenges abound. The decentralized nature of the

dark web makes copyright enforcement complex, and malicious actors sometimes exploit fan enthusiasm for scams or illegal activities. This necessitates vigilance and critical thinking before engaging with any content or community.

Ultimately, the realm of unofficial fan content on the dark web presents a double-edged sword. While harbouring the risk of copyright infringement and ethical dilemmas, it also fosters a vibrant community of passionate creators, empowers diverse voices, and pushes the boundaries of creative expression. Approaching this realm with respect, responsible engagement, and a strong moral compass is crucial to navigating its complexities and harnessing its potential for positive creative exploration.

PART X: HUMANITARIAN EFFORTS

CHAPTER 46: SECURE COMMUNICATION FOR HUMAN RIGHTS ACTIVISTS – WHISPERS IN THE SHADOWS, VOICES FOR CHANGE

Our exploration of the dark web takes a turn towards a realm of vital importance: secure communication for human rights activists. Imagine a hidden network, its pathways not paved with data, but with whispered messages and encrypted exchanges. Here, activists operating under oppressive regimes, whistle-blowers exposing corporate wrongdoing, and journalists facing censorship find a glimmer of hope – the ability to communicate securely and advocate for change in the face of adversity.

The need for such secure channels arises from the harsh realities faced by those fighting for human rights. In countries with restrictive regimes, dissent can be met with imprisonment, violence, or even death. Journalists face intimidation and surveillance, making it difficult to report freely. Whistle-blowers fear retaliation for exposing wrongdoing. The dark web, with its inherent anonymity and encryption layers, offers a potential solution, albeit not without its challenges.

Let us begin by acknowledging the risks and ethical considerations. The dark web, while providing anonymity, harbours criminal activities and malicious actors. Navigating this hidden space requires caution and awareness of potential scams and dangers. Additionally, relying solely on the dark web for communication might create echo chambers, hindering collaboration with mainstream channels and broader audiences.

However, the benefits for human rights defenders are undeniable. Platforms offering encrypted messaging, secure file sharing, and even collaborative tools empower activists to connect, share information, and strategize without fear of interception or surveillance. This fosters international collaboration, empowers marginalized voices, and enables the documentation of human rights abuses.

One powerful example lies in the use of the dark web by journalists operating under repressive regimes. By communicating securely with sources and sharing sensitive information anonymously, they can continue their vital work of exposing corruption and holding oppressive regimes accountable. Similarly, whistle-blowers can safely report wrongdoing without jeopardizing their safety or careers.

But the story doesn't end there. The dark web also facilitates communication and collaboration between activists across borders, fostering solidarity and amplifying their voices on a global scale. This allows for the sharing of best practices, coordination of efforts, and the mobilization of international support for human rights campaigns.

However, challenges remain. Accessing and navigating the

dark web requires technical expertise, not readily available to all activists. Additionally, the decentralized nature of the dark web makes identifying reliable platforms and trustworthy individuals difficult, demanding careful research and verification.

Ultimately, the dark web presents a complex landscape for human rights activists. While harbouring risks and demanding responsible use, it offers a vital tool for secure communication, international collaboration, and amplifying voices for change. Approaching this realm with caution, technical preparation, and a strong understanding of its complexities is crucial for harnessing its potential for positive social impact.

CHAPTER 47: PLANNING AND ORGANIZING PROTESTS

The anonymity and vastness of the dark web have facilitated a range of activities, from the nefarious to the noble. Among its more virtuous uses is the organization of protests against oppressive regimes, policies, or injustices where conventional digital platforms are heavily monitored or censored. This chapter delves into how activists harness the dark web for planning and organizing protests, outlining the strategies employed, the challenges faced, and the ethical considerations that come into play.

The dark web, a part of the internet that is not indexed by traditional search engines and requires specific software, configurations, or authorization to access, provides a veil of anonymity for its users. This anonymity is crucial for activists and dissenters in countries or regions where freedom of speech is restricted, and surveillance is rampant. The initial step in organizing a protest via the dark web involves establishing a secure communication channel. Activists often use encrypted messaging services that are accessible on the dark web to coordinate their efforts without the fear of interception by authorities.

Once a secure channel is established, the next phase is recruitment and mobilization. Recruitment is typically done through forums and chat rooms that are dedicated to political activism, human rights, or specific causes. These platforms allow organizers to disseminate information about the protest, including its objectives, the logistics of the gathering, and any preparations participants should make. Mobilization, on the other hand, requires a more nuanced approach. It involves not only rallying support but also ensuring that the protest remains peaceful and does not endanger the participants. Organizers often distribute guides on non-violent resistance, legal rights, and safety measures for dealing with law enforcement.

The planning phase is critical and involves meticulous attention to detail. Organizers must decide on the protest's location, timing, and duration, taking into account the potential response from authorities. They must also plan for contingencies, such as what to do if the protest is forcibly dispersed. Logistics, such as the provision of medical aid, legal assistance, and communication among participants during the protest, are also organized through the dark web. This phase often involves collaboration with sympathetic NGOs or international bodies that can offer support or observe the protest to ensure human rights are respected.

The ethical considerations of using the dark web for protest organizations are complex. On one hand, it empowers citizens to stand up against oppression and injustice in a relatively safe manner. On the other hand, the anonymity of the dark web can also shield individuals with malicious intent, who may seek to hijack peaceful protests for their ends or incite violence. Organizers must be vigilant and establish clear codes of conduct for participants, emphasizing the peaceful nature of the protest and the importance of respecting public and private property.

The challenges faced by organizers are manifold. They must

navigate the technical complexities of the dark web, ensuring secure and anonymous communication channels. They also face the constant threat of infiltration by state actors or counter-protest groups who may seek to disrupt the protest or harm participants. Additionally, the reliance on digital communication means there is always a risk of misinformation or communication breakdowns, which can lead to chaos during the actual event.

Despite these challenges, the dark web has proven to be an invaluable tool for activists around the world. The Arab Spring and the Hong Kong protests are notable examples where digital platforms, including parts of the dark web, played a pivotal role in organizing and galvanizing support. These protests not only brought global attention to the causes they championed but also demonstrated the power of the internet as a tool for social change.

In conclusion, the use of the dark web for planning and organizing protests is a testament to the resilience and ingenuity of activists in the face of oppression. While it presents ethical dilemmas and significant challenges, the dark web offers a platform for peaceful resistance and the fight for justice that is difficult to replicate in the visible digital world. As technology evolves, so too will the strategies of those who seek to use it for the greater good, ensuring that the flame of protest burns bright even in the darkest corners of the internet.

CHAPTER 48: DISCREET FUNDRAISING FOR JUST CAUSES - WALKING THE ETHICAL TIGHTROPE

Our exploration of the shadows unfolds into a realm imbued with moral complexity: discreet fundraising for just causes. Imagine a hidden network, not paved with coins, but with whispered pleas for support, cloaked in anonymity for reasons both noble and unsettling. Here, we encounter individuals and groups seeking funding for causes deemed controversial, unconventional, or even illegal on the surface web, raising both ethical questions and highlighting the nuances of navigating sensitive territory.

Before venturing deeper, let's dispel a misconception: not all discreet fundraising on the dark web falls into the criminal domain. Many legitimate causes operate underground due to limitations imposed by their geographical location, political climate, or the nature of their activities. Imagine whistle-blowers seeking resources to expose corporate wrongdoing, activists raising funds to combat oppressive regimes, or persecuted groups financing their fight for basic human rights.

However, the shadows also harbour ventures pushing the boundaries of legality and ethics. Groups raising funds for illegal operations, individuals crowdfunding for harmful activities, or even extremists seeking financial support for their agendas paint a darker picture. Navigating this complex ethical landscape requires discernment and an understanding of the potential risks involved.

The primary reason for utilizing the dark web for fundraising often relates to anonymity. Donors seeking discretion for personal or security reasons, organizations operating under restrictive regimes, or causes deemed controversial in their societies find a platform here. Yet, anonymity necessitates due diligence. Platforms often rely on escrow services, holding funds until goals are met and promises are fulfilled. However, the reliability and security of these services vary greatly, demanding meticulous research and verification from potential contributors.

Beyond ethical considerations, practical challenges abound. Transactions primarily rely on cryptocurrencies, susceptible to volatility and scams. The decentralized nature of the dark web makes legal oversight complex, further emphasizing the need for individual responsibility and risk assessment before contributing to any campaign.

Despite the inherent risks, legitimate and impactful projects also flourish. Journalists seeking funding to expose corruption, activists raising awareness for marginalized communities, or even researchers requiring resources for unconventional research projects find a platform on the dark web. This highlights the potential for this hidden domain to support valuable initiatives beyond the limitations of traditional fundraising models.

One intriguing aspect of this realm is the emergence

of "dark DAOs" – Decentralized Autonomous Organizations utilizing blockchain technology for transparent and equitable distribution of funds. These self-governing structures raise promising possibilities for anonymous yet accountable fundraising but also introduce complex legal and technological questions demanding careful consideration.

Ultimately, discreet fundraising on the dark web presents a paradox. While harbouring risks and ethical dilemmas, it offers a platform for unconventional ventures, fosters innovation beyond traditional limitations, and empowers individuals and groups seeking funding outside the mainstream. Approaching this realm with critical thinking, a strong moral compass, and a deep understanding of potential pitfalls is crucial to navigating its complexities and mitigating the risks while harnessing its potential for positive social impact.

CHAPTER 49: REPORTING HUMAN RIGHTS ABUSES ANONYMOUSLY - WHISPERS IN THE DARK, HOPE FOR JUSTICE

Our exploration of the dark web delves into a realm with profound implications for human rights: anonymous reporting of abuses. Imagine a hidden network, its pathways not paved with data, but with whispered testimonies, cloaked in anonymity to expose injustice and seek accountability. While fraught with ethical complexities and practical challenges, this domain carries the potential to empower voices silenced by fear and oppression.

Before venturing deeper, let us acknowledge the ethical considerations. Anonymity, while protecting whistle-blowers and victims, can hinder investigations and create difficulties in verifying information. Malicious actors may exploit this anonymity for disinformation or personal vendettas. It is crucial to approach anonymous reports with critical thinking and robust verification processes.

Now, imagine the harsh realities faced by those fighting for human rights. In oppressive regimes, speaking out can lead to imprisonment, torture, or even death. Whistle-blowers fear retaliation from powerful entities. Victims of abuse may lack the resources or support to publicly denounce their experiences. The dark web, with its potential for anonymity, offers a glimmer of hope, a platform for reporting abuses without fear of reprisal.

Platforms on the dark web offer encrypted messaging, secure file sharing, and whistle-blower hotlines. Individuals can anonymously report human rights abuses, share evidence, and connect with journalists, activists, or legal professionals working to expose injustices and hold perpetrators accountable. This empowers marginalized voices, fosters international collaboration, and documents human rights violations for future action.

Consider the example of journalists operating under repressive regimes. By anonymously submitting sensitive information through dark web platforms, they can expose corruption, document human rights abuses, and hold authorities accountable without endangering themselves or their sources. Similarly, whistle-blowers can reveal wrongdoing within corporations or organizations without fearing professional repercussions.

However, challenges abound. Verifying the authenticity of anonymous reports requires meticulous effort. Platforms must implement robust verification mechanisms to combat disinformation and ensure the legitimacy of whistle-blowers' claims. Additionally, navigating the dark web requires technical expertise, not readily available to all potential whistle-blowers or investigators.

Moreover, legal complexities arise. The legality of anonymously reporting abuses varies by jurisdiction, and navigating international legal frameworks can be challenging. Whistle-blowers and platforms must operate within legal boundaries and seek legal counsel when necessary.

Ultimately, anonymous reporting on the dark web presents a double-edged sword. While harbouring risks and demanding responsible use, it offers a vital tool for empowering silenced voices, exposing injustices, and seeking accountability for human rights abuses. Approaching this realm with caution, robust verification practices, and a deep understanding of the legal landscape is crucial to maximize its potential for positive impact while mitigating the inherent risks.

CHAPTER 50: ANONYMOUS CHARITY - GIVING IN THE SHADOWS, SHINING A LIGHT ON LIVES

Our final expedition on the dark web takes us to a realm driven by compassion and selflessness: anonymous charity. Imagine a hidden network, paved not with coins, but with whispered acts of generosity, cloaked in secrecy to empower both donors and recipients. While fraught with practical challenges and ethical considerations, this shadowy space offers a unique platform for those seeking to give without fanfare or expectation of recognition.

Before venturing deeper, let us acknowledge the potential pitfalls. Anonymity, while protecting donor privacy, can hinder transparency and accountability. Malicious actors may exploit this anonymity for fraudulent schemes or money laundering. It is crucial to approach anonymous donation platforms with due diligence and ensure their legitimacy and responsible operation.

Now, imagine the diverse motivations for seeking anonymity

in giving. Individuals may wish to protect their privacy due to cultural norms, religious beliefs, or fear of social pressure. Donors in countries with restrictive regimes may fear persecution for supporting certain causes. Additionally, some may simply prefer the act of giving to be a personal expression of compassion, devoid of external validation.

Platforms on the dark web offer various options for anonymous donations. Cryptocurrency transactions enable anonymity, and platforms often utilize escrow services to hold funds until designated charities receive them and confirm their legitimacy. This empowers individuals to support diverse causes, from established organizations to smaller grassroots initiatives, while maintaining their privacy.

Consider the example of individuals living under oppressive regimes. Through anonymous donations on the dark web, they can support persecuted communities, human rights organizations, or independent journalists fighting for freedom and justice without attracting unwanted attention. Additionally, individuals struggling financially themselves might anonymously donate small amounts to help others in need, fostering a sense of community and mutual support.

However, challenges abound beyond ethical considerations. Verifying the legitimacy of donation platforms and recipient charities on the dark web requires extra effort. Donors must research platforms thoroughly, scrutinize their operations, and seek independent verification measures to avoid scams or fraudulent activities.

Moreover, legal complexities arise. Depending on the jurisdiction and regulations surrounding cryptocurrency transactions and anonymous donations, legal considerations become crucial. Donors and platforms must operate within legal boundaries and seek legal counsel when necessary to ensure responsible and compliant donation practices.

Ultimately, anonymous charity on the dark web presents a complex landscape. While harbouring risks and demanding vigilance, it offers a unique platform for individuals seeking to express their compassion and philanthropy discreetly, empowering both donors and recipients in unique ways. Approaching this realm with caution, meticulous research, and a strong commitment to ethical giving is crucial to navigate its complexities and maximize its potential for positive social impact.

PART XI: OVERCOMING CHALLENGES

CHAPTER 51: DARK WEB'S FIGHT AGAINST CHILD EXPLOITATION

The dark web, often depicted as a lawless frontier teeming with nefarious activities, harbours within its depths a less publicized but equally potent force for good. Among its commendable endeavours is the fight against child exploitation, a scourge that unfortunately finds a shadowy refuge online. This chapter ventures into how the dark web becomes an unexpected ally in combating child exploitation, highlighting the collaborative efforts of activists, non-profit organizations, and law enforcement agencies to shield the most vulnerable.

The battle against child exploitation on the dark web is waged on multiple fronts, employing a combination of sophisticated technology, human intelligence, and cross-border cooperation. The inherent anonymity of the dark web, while a boon for privacy advocates and political dissidents, also presents significant challenges for those working to protect children. It's this anonymity that has allowed certain areas of the dark web to become havens for the distribution of child exploitation material. However, this same anonymity can be turned against those who perpetrate these crimes, providing a cover for operations aimed at dismantling their networks.

Technological Warfare

At the forefront of this battle is the deployment of cutting-edge technology. Artificial intelligence (AI) and machine learning algorithms are increasingly utilized to scan the dark web for material related to child exploitation. These tools can analyse vast amounts of data at unprecedented speeds, identifying patterns and connections that would be impossible for human investigators to discern in a reasonable timeframe. Blockchain technology also plays a role, in tracking cryptocurrency transactions that are often used to finance illegal activities, leading to the identification and apprehension of perpetrators.

Collaborative Networks

The fight against child exploitation on the dark web is characterized by an extensive collaborative network that spans continents. Non-profit organizations, such as the Internet Watch Foundation (IWF) and the National Centre for Missing & Exploited Children (NCMEC), work tirelessly to identify and remove content that exploits children. These organizations also maintain hotlines that allow individuals to report anonymously any illegal material they encounter online.

Law enforcement agencies across the globe have intensified their efforts to combat child exploitation on the dark web. Operations such as the takedown of the Playpen site in 2015, one of the largest hidden services for child exploitation material, underscore the potential for success. Such operations often require coordination among different countries' law enforcement agencies, facilitated by entities like Europol and Interpol. These collaborative efforts are crucial, given the borderless nature of the internet and the jurisdictional challenges it presents.

Educational Initiatives

Prevention through education is another critical aspect of the fight against child exploitation. Organizations and activists use the dark web not only to track and report illegal activities but also to educate the public about the dangers children face online.

Through forums and encrypted messaging services, they share information on how to protect children from online predators, recognize signs of exploitation, and report concerns safely and anonymously.

Ethical and Legal Challenges

The battle against child exploitation on the dark web is fraught with ethical and legal challenges. The use of hacking tools and surveillance software by law enforcement to infiltrate illegal networks raises concerns about privacy and the potential for abuse. Moreover, the risk of false positives—misidentifying innocent activities as illegal—can have devastating effects on individuals mistakenly caught in the crossfire.

Despite these challenges, the consensus remains that the fight against child exploitation must continue, with safeguards in place to prevent abuses of power. Transparency, oversight, and adherence to legal standards are emphasized to ensure that the pursuit of justice does not infringe upon fundamental human rights.

Looking Forward

As technology evolves, so too do the tactics of those who exploit children. The fight against child exploitation on the dark web is an ongoing battle, requiring constant vigilance, adaptation, and international cooperation. Innovations in technology offer new tools for both protectors and perpetrators, making it a perpetual arms race.

The dark web's role in fighting child exploitation highlights a complex reality: a domain of the internet often vilified for its hidden dangers also serves as a critical battleground for protecting the innocent. The efforts of dedicated individuals and organizations, working in the shadows to cast light on those who harm, remind us of the power of collective action in confronting and overcoming the darkest aspects of human behaviour.

In conclusion, the dark web's fight against child exploitation is a testament to the resilience of the human spirit, the ingenuity of those committed to defending the vulnerable, and the necessity of global collaboration. It's a stark reminder that within the depths of the internet's most hidden corners, there are beacons of hope and forces for good, tirelessly working to ensure a safer world for all children.

CHAPTER 52: SHINING A LIGHT ON DARKNESS - REPORTING AND TRACKING ILLEGAL ACTIVITIES

Our exploration of the dark web continues with a critical aspect: its potential role in reporting and tracking illegal activities. Imagine hidden alleys transformed into information pathways, whispers evolving into actionable intelligence. While acknowledging the ethical complexities and inherent difficulties, we delve into the realm where darkness itself can be harnessed to shed light on criminal enterprises and harmful agendas.

Before venturing deeper, let's address the ethical considerations. Engaging with the dark web, even for noble purposes, necessitates caution and awareness of potential risks. Infiltrating criminal networks might raise legal questions, and navigating information ethically demands careful discernment. Collaboration with law enforcement remains crucial, ensuring responsible action and avoiding entrapment or vigilantism.

Now, envision the challenges faced by law enforcement agencies in combating cybercrime. Traditional methods often struggle to penetrate the encrypted anonymity of the dark web. Yet, this hidden sphere also harbours traces of illegal activity and breadcrumbs left behind in online forums, marketplaces, and communication channels. By venturing into this digital underbelly, researchers and ethical hackers can gather valuable intelligence, expose criminal networks, track illicit activities, and ultimately aid in bringing perpetrators to justice.

Consider, for instance, the collaboration between ethical hackers and law enforcement agencies to infiltrate and dismantle online drug marketplaces. By analysing data and communication patterns, they identify key players, gather evidence, and disrupt illegal operations. Similarly, tracking financial transactions on the dark web can expose money laundering schemes and identify criminal organizations profiting from human trafficking or arms sales.

However, challenges abound beyond ethical considerations. Anonymity, while shielding criminals, also hinders investigations. Verifying information gleaned from the dark web requires meticulous effort, and infiltrating online groups carries inherent risks. Additionally, legal complexities arise, requiring careful navigation of international jurisdictions and cybercrime laws.

Moreover, the dark web constantly evolves, demanding continuous adaptation and technical expertise. Law enforcement agencies and researchers must stay vigilant, develop sophisticated data analysis tools, and foster collaboration with ethical hackers and cybersecurity experts.

Ultimately, shining a light on illegal activities within the dark web presents a complex and evolving landscape. While harbouring risks and demanding ethical responsibility, it offers a valuable tool for law enforcement and researchers in the fight against cybercrime. Approaching this realm with meticulous caution, collaboration with authorities, and a commitment to legal and ethical frameworks are crucial to maximising its potential for positive impact and ensuring the darkness does not continue to harbour unseen harm.

CHAPTER 53: DIGITAL HYGIENE: NAVIGATING THE SHADOWLANDS SAFELY

As our exploration of the dark web draws to a close, we must address the crucial aspect of personal safety and responsible engagement. Venturing into these hidden digital spaces requires a heightened awareness of potential risks and meticulous adherence to digital hygiene practices. Remember, venturing into the dark web is similar to exploring uncharted territory; preparation and caution are paramount.

Before immersing yourself, acknowledge the inherent risks. Malicious actors lurk in the shadows, ready to exploit vulnerabilities. Malware infections, phishing scams, and identity theft are common threats. Additionally, exposure to illegal or disturbing content can be traumatizing. Approaching the dark web with the same caution you would exercise in dangerous physical environments is vital.

Now, imagine equipping yourself with this digital expedition. Your first line of defence is a robust security shield. Utilize high-quality antivirus and anti-malware software, ensure your operating system is updated with the latest security patches, and consider using a virtual machine specifically for dark web exploration. Strong, unique passwords for all accounts and two-factor authentication wherever possible are essential.

Next, consider anonymity tools with caution. While Tor offers some level of anonymity, it's not fool proof. Virtual Private Networks (VPNs) may not provide complete protection and can have legal implications depending on your location. Remember, true anonymity on the dark web is challenging, and responsible behaviour remains paramount.

Furthermore, navigate with prudence. Avoid clicking on suspicious links, downloading unknown files, or engaging with untrusted individuals. Remember, if something seems too good to be true, it probably is. Exercise critical thinking and healthy scepticism towards all information encountered.

Remember, communication carries risks. Avoid sharing personal information or engaging in activities that could put yourself or others at risk. If you encounter illegal activity, report it immediately to the appropriate authorities. Remember, you are not a vigilante; safety and legality are paramount.

Finally, emerge cautiously. After leaving the dark web, clear your browsing history, cookies, and cache. Scan your system for malware and update your passwords again. Remember, digital hygiene is an ongoing process, not a one-time event.

While the dark web harbours risks, responsible individuals can navigate it with caution and utilize its potential for good. Remember, ethical engagement, meticulous digital hygiene practices, and collaboration with established authorities are key to maximizing the positive impact and minimizing the inherent dangers. Always prioritize your safety and legal compliance; venturing into the dark web is not for the faint of heart.

CHAPTER 54: LEGAL LABYRINTH AND UNCHARTED HORIZONS - THE FUTURE OF THE DARK WEB

As our expedition through the shadows concludes, we arrive at a crucial crossroads: the complex legal landscape surrounding the dark web and its uncertain future. Imagine a hidden network, not paved with data, but with questions and uncertainties. While acknowledging its potential for good, we must confront the legal challenges that both constrain and shape its evolution.

Before venturing deeper, let us acknowledge the legal complexities. The anonymity offered by the dark web presents a double-edged sword. While protecting individuals from oppressive regimes or enabling whistle-blowers, it also harbours illegal activities like drug trafficking, cybercrime, and money laundering. Navigating this legal minefield requires a nuanced understanding of international jurisdictions, evolving cybercrime laws, and the ethical implications of various activities.

Now, imagine the challenges faced by law enforcement agencies. Prosecuting crimes committed on the dark web proves difficult due to the anonymity and decentralized nature of the network. Identifying perpetrators, gathering evidence, and securing international cooperation are complex tasks. Additionally, balancing the need for security with individual privacy rights remains a constant struggle.

Consider, for instance, the ongoing debate surrounding encryption. While crucial for protecting individual privacy, it also hinders law enforcement investigations. Finding a balance between these competing interests is a delicate act, requiring ongoing dialogue and innovative solutions.

However, the future holds potential for progress. Technological advancements like blockchain technology offer opportunities for creating more transparent and accountable dark web platforms, while law enforcement agencies are developing sophisticated data analysis tools and fostering collaboration with ethical hackers and cybersecurity experts.

Furthermore, legal frameworks are evolving to address the unique challenges posed by the dark web. International cooperation is increasing, and new laws are being drafted to combat cybercrime and hold perpetrators accountable. This ongoing legal evolution is crucial for ensuring a safer and more responsible digital landscape.

Ultimately, the future of the dark web remains uncertain. While its potential for good cannot be ignored, its inherent risks demand careful consideration and responsible action. Legal frameworks must adapt, technology must evolve ethically, and individuals must navigate this complex space with caution and awareness. Whether it becomes a haven for innovation and social good or a breeding ground for illegal activities remains to be seen.

CHAPTER 55: LESSONS FROM SHUTDOWNS: SILK ROAD AND BEYOND

Our exploration wouldn't be complete without examining the fate of notorious dark web marketplaces like Silk Road. Its 2013 shutdown by the FBI sent shockwaves through the online underworld, sparking questions about the effectiveness of such actions and the long-term impact on the dark web ecosystem.

Silk Road wasn't the first, nor the last, major dark web marketplace to be shut down. Hydra Market, known for its massive user base and diverse illegal offerings, met its demise in 2022 through a joint operation by German and US authorities. However, these takedowns often resemble whack-a-mole, with new platforms quickly emerging to fill the void.

But shutdowns also offer valuable lessons. Silk Road's closure, while disrupting illegal activity, did not eliminate it. Law enforcement resources are limited, and the decentralized nature of the dark web makes complete eradication nearly impossible. Instead, a focus on disrupting financial infrastructure, identifying key players, and fostering international collaboration might prove more effective in the long run.

Furthermore, shutdowns can have unintended consequences.

By driving users to smaller, less regulated platforms, they might inadvertently increase risks for both buyers and sellers. Additionally, restricting access to information and resources on the dark web, even those with legitimate uses, can have negative impacts on marginalized communities and individuals operating under oppressive regimes.

The future of the dark web remains uncertain. Technological advancements, evolving legal frameworks, and ongoing law enforcement efforts will undoubtedly shape its trajectory. Whether it becomes a haven for innovation and social good or a breeding ground for illegal activities depends not just on technology and law, but on the choices we make as individuals and societies. By fostering responsible engagement, advocating for ethical technologies, and supporting transparent legal frameworks, we can shape the future of the dark web to be a force for good rather than a cause for concern.

PART XII:
UNDERSTANDING
DIVERSE
COMMUNITIES

CHAPTER 56: RELIGIOUS COMMUNITIES UNDER REPRESSION

In the shadowed corridors of the dark web, where anonymity reigns and the global digital gaze rarely penetrates, a surprising and profoundly human narrative unfolds. This is the story of religious communities under repression, for whom the dark web has become a sanctuary, a place of gathering, and a beacon of hope. Far from the mainstream portrayal of the dark web as a den of iniquity, this chapter explores its role as a lifeline for those seeking to practice their faith free from persecution.

Sanctuary in the Shadows

In regions where religious expression is tightly controlled or outright banned, the dark web offers a discreet platform for the exchange of ideas, worship, and fellowship. Encrypted services and forums serve as digital churches, mosques, synagogues, and temples, providing a space where the faithful can congregate without fear of discovery. Here, users from around the globe share religious texts, engage in discussions, and support one another in their spiritual journeys, all under the protective cloak of anonymity.

The Digital Silk Road of Faith

The dark web has evolved into a modern-day Silk Road, not of spices and silk, but of spiritual sustenance. It facilitates the smuggling of digital religious materials into countries where such texts are censored or banned. Bibles, Qur'ans, Talmuds, and other sacred texts, often translated into local languages, are discreetly distributed, offering spiritual nourishment to those starved of religious freedom. This digital dissemination of religious content is revolutionary, breaking down barriers imposed by oppressive regimes and challenging the control they wield over spiritual expression.

Empowering the Persecuted

Beyond providing spiritual resources, the dark web empowers persecuted religious communities by offering platforms for organization and advocacy. Encrypted messaging apps and forums allow for the planning of peaceful gatherings, educational seminars, and support networks without the prying eyes of hostile governments. These digital havens also serve as critical channels for disseminating information about human rights abuses, drawing international attention to the plight of oppressed religious groups, and mobilizing global support.

Challenges and Ethical Dilemmas

However, the use of the dark web by religious communities is not without its challenges and ethical dilemmas. The anonymity that protects also poses a risk, as extremist groups may exploit these platforms to spread hateful ideologies or plan violent acts. Thus, moderators of religious forums on the dark web often find themselves in a delicate balancing act, striving to maintain a safe space for genuine seekers and worshippers while guarding against infiltration by those with malicious intent.

Moreover, the reliance on the dark web for religious freedom raises questions about digital literacy and access. For many in repressed communities, the technical knowledge required to navigate the dark web safely is a barrier, limiting the reach of these digital sanctuaries. Efforts to educate potential users about secure browsing practices are critical to ensuring that the benefits of the dark web are accessible to all who need it.

Testimonies of Hope

Amidst the adversity faced by repressed religious communities, the dark web has become a testament to human resilience and the enduring quest for spiritual freedom. Testimonies from users who have found solace and community through these digital platforms are poignant reminders of the dark web's potential for good. From a Christian in North Korea sharing prayers with believers across the world, to a Muslim woman in Iran accessing scholarly works on Islam, the stories of faith thriving in the face of oppression are both inspiring and humbling.

The Road Ahead

As technology advances and the digital landscape evolves, the role of the dark web in supporting religious communities under repression will undoubtedly change. The ongoing challenge for these communities, and for the activists and technologists who support them, is to stay one step ahead of those who seek to silence them. Ensuring the safety, accessibility, and effectiveness of these digital sanctuaries remains a paramount concern.

In conclusion, the story of religious communities finding refuge on the dark web is a powerful narrative of adaptation, resilience, and hope. It challenges prevailing perceptions of the dark web, revealing its capacity to serve not only as a space for anonymity but as a force for spiritual freedom and human connection. As we journey through the digital age, the expeditionary tale of faith flourishing in the shadows continues to unfold, a beacon of light in the darkness, reminding us of the indomitable nature of the human spirit in its quest for the divine.

CHAPTER 57: POLITICALLY SUPPRESSED INDIVIDUALS AND GROUPS

In the labyrinthine depths of the dark web, beyond the reach of conventional scrutiny, lies a sanctuary for the politically oppressed. This chapter embarks on an exploration of how the dark web serves as a bastion for those whose voices are stifled, where dissidents, whistle-blowers, and politically suppressed groups find refuge and a means to fight for freedom and democracy.

The Veil of Anonymity

At the heart of the dark web's appeal to politically suppressed individuals is its provision of anonymity. This digital veil shields users from the prying eyes of authoritarian regimes, allowing them to speak, organize, and mobilize without fear of retribution. Here, encrypted communication services become the lifeblood of political activism, ensuring that messages, plans, and data are shared securely.

Forums of Freedom

The dark web hosts a plethora of forums and chat rooms

dedicated to political discourse and activism. These platforms enable suppressed voices to exchange ideas, disseminate information censored by their governments, and coordinate actions. For many, it's a digital agora where the ideals of democracy and freedom are kept alive amidst external repression. The stories shared within these forums not only offer solidarity and hope but also serve as a powerful testament to the human spirit's resilience.

Safe Havens for Whistle-blowers

Whistle-blowers, who risk everything to expose corruption, injustice, and violations of human rights, find a haven in the dark web. Platforms like SecureDrop and GlobaLeaks cater specifically to these individuals, enabling them to submit sensitive information anonymously. This information often finds its way to journalists and news outlets, bypassing government censorship and reaching the global stage. The impact of such revelations can be profound, sparking public outrage, policy changes, and even the toppling of corrupt officials.

Liberating the Silenced Press

In countries where the press is shackled by state control, the dark web offers a clandestine route for journalists to report the truth. Independent news outlets operate in the shadows, publishing stories that would otherwise be suppressed. These digital publications not only inform the local populace but also attract international attention to injustices that might have remained hidden.

Challenges and Complexities

Operating within the dark web, however, is fraught with complexities. The anonymity that protects users also opens the door to surveillance, hacking, and misinformation by the very forces they seek to evade. Navigating this digital underworld requires technical savvy, constant vigilance, and a deep understanding of digital security practices. Furthermore, the ethical dilemma of using a platform known for illicit activities cannot be ignored, raising questions about the means to an end.

Global Connectivity and Solidarity

One of the most significant aspects of the dark web for politically suppressed groups is its ability to connect them with a global network of supporters. Through crowdfunding platforms and social media channels hidden from the mainstream internet, these groups can secure financial, logistical, and moral support. International NGOs and human rights organizations also use the dark web to coordinate with activists on the ground, providing them with resources, training, and international platforms to voice their struggles.

Testimonies of Resistance

The narratives emerging from the dark web are powerful and poignant. From the dissident in Belarus sharing real-time updates on government crackdowns to the feminist collective in Saudi Arabia discussing gender equality, the dark web is replete with stories of courage and defiance. These accounts not only document the realities of political suppression but also inspire a broader movement towards global awareness and action against oppression.

The Future of Digital Dissidence

As technology evolves, so too will the strategies of both oppressors and the oppressed. The arms race between surveillance and privacy continues to escalate, with both sides developing more sophisticated tools. The resilience of politically suppressed individuals and groups, supported by the dark web, highlights a fundamental truth: the human yearning for freedom cannot be extinguished, and the fight for rights and justice will adapt to every challenge.

In conclusion, the dark web's role in supporting politically suppressed individuals and groups is a testament to the indomitable desire for freedom and justice. It represents a double-edged sword, offering protection and a voice to those who would otherwise be silenced, yet requiring a careful navigation of its inherent risks. The expedition into the dark web's role in political activism reveals not only the complexities of digital resistance but also the enduring power of human solidarity. As we continue to explore the multifaceted landscape of the dark web, we uncover the relentless pursuit of democracy and freedom, lighting a path through the darkness for oppressed voices around the world.

CHAPTER 58: AMPLIFYING VOICES: MINORITY COMMUNITIES AND THE DARK WEB

As we delve deeper into the hidden corners of the digital world, we encounter a phenomenon brimming with potential and nuance: minority communities utilizing the dark web to find their voice and connect with others. Imagine a hidden network, not paved with data, but with whispered dialogues and shared experiences, offering marginalized groups a platform for expression and community in an often hostile world.

Before venturing into this realm, it's crucial to acknowledge the complexities. While offering a potential haven for marginalized voices, the dark web harbours risks and necessitates responsible engagement. Anonymity, while granting privacy, can be exploited for malicious purposes. Malicious actors might infiltrate forums, spread misinformation, or even pose safety threats. Navigating this space requires caution, critical thinking, and a strong emphasis on safety.

Now, imagine the challenges faced by individuals and communities whose voices are often silenced or suppressed. In countries with restrictive regimes, LGBTQ+ individuals fearing persecution, ethnic minorities facing discrimination, or activists fighting for marginalized groups often lack safe spaces for open communication and community building. The dark web, with its inherent anonymity, offers a glimmer of hope, a platform for fostering connections, sharing experiences, and finding solace in solidarity.

Consider, for instance, online forums dedicated to LGBTQ+ communities in countries with strict anti-homosexuality laws. These forums provide a safe space for individuals to connect, share stories, and access information vital to their well-being. Similarly, religious minorities facing persecution can utilize the dark web to organize, document human rights abuses, and connect with international support networks.

However, challenges abound beyond potential risks. Accessing and navigating the dark web requires technical expertise, not readily available to all individuals within marginalized communities. Additionally, verifying the legitimacy of platforms and users within these forums can be difficult, demanding careful research and discernment.

Furthermore, legal considerations loom large. While activities on the dark web might be legal in some regions, they might violate laws in others, placing users at risk. Understanding legal frameworks and prioritizing personal safety remains paramount.

But despite the challenges, the potential for positive impact shines through. The dark web has empowered marginalized communities to:

Find and build communities: Individuals facing isolation due to their identity or beliefs can connect with others who share their experiences, fostering a sense of belonging and support.
Share information and resources: Forums on the dark web can serve as hubs for sharing vital information on topics like LGBTQ + rights, safe havens for religious minorities, or resources for

advocating for marginalized groups.

Organize and mobilize: The dark web can facilitate communication and collaboration between activists working on behalf of marginalized communities, enabling them to plan actions, raise awareness, and hold authorities accountable.

Document human rights abuses: Individuals facing persecution can anonymously document human rights violations, providing valuable evidence for advocacy efforts and international pressure on oppressive regimes.

Ultimately, the dark web presents a double-edged sword for marginalized communities. While harbouring risks and demanding responsible engagement, it offers a unique platform for amplifying voices, fostering connections, and advocating for change. Approaching this realm with caution, prioritizing safety, and legal compliance, and harnessing the power of technology ethically are crucial to maximizing its potential for positive impact on marginalized communities worldwide.

CHAPTER 59: WHISPERS OF HERITAGE: PRESERVING ENDANGERED CULTURES ON THE DARK WEB

Our exploration of the shadowy corners of the web leads us to a realm steeped in tradition and identity: the use of the dark web for ethnic and cultural preservation. Imagine hidden pathways, not paved with data, but with echoes of ancestral languages, whispers of forgotten customs, and a digital ark safeguarding endangered heritage. While acknowledging the inherent complexities and ethical considerations, we delve into the potential of this hidden sphere to empower communities and bridge the digital divide for cultural survival.

Before venturing deeper, let us address the ethical considerations. Anonymity, while safeguarding cultural knowledge from suppression or exploitation, can harbour malicious actors seeking to distort traditions or misuse sensitive information. Additionally, accessibility remains a challenge, creating potential inequalities within communities and raising concerns about cultural appropriation. Navigating this space requires ethical responsibility, community-driven approaches, and a focus on ensuring equitable access to cultural heritage.

Now, imagine the challenges faced by communities struggling to preserve their cultural identities in the face of globalization, assimilation, and political repression. Indigenous languages fading away due to dominant cultures, traditional knowledge threatened by economic pressures, and artistic expressions facing censorship all paint a stark picture. The dark web, with its potential for anonymity and decentralized storage, offers a glimmer of hope, a platform for safeguarding heritage and empowering communities to take control of their cultural narratives.

Consider, for instance, indigenous communities utilizing the dark web to document and share their languages in interactive online dictionaries. These platforms not only preserve vital linguistic heritage but also empower future generations to reconnect with their ancestral tongues. Similarly, groups facing cultural oppression might use the dark web to archive traditional music, art, and literature, ensuring their survival beyond the reach of censorship.

However, challenges abound beyond ethical considerations. Technical expertise for accessing and utilizing the dark web is often limited within traditional communities, creating a digital divide, and hindering wider participation. Additionally, verifying the authenticity and accuracy of information shared on the dark web requires scrutiny to avoid misinformation and cultural distortion.

Furthermore, legal complexities arise. Cultural heritage, particularly intellectual property rights surrounding traditional knowledge or artistic expressions, often falls under complex legal frameworks. Understanding and respecting these frameworks is crucial to avoid unintended legal consequences.

Despite the challenges, the potential for positive impact shines through. The dark web has empowered communities to:

Document and archive cultural heritage: Languages, traditional knowledge, artistic expressions, and historical records can be safely stored and shared, ensuring their survival for future generations.

Promote cultural revitalization: Platforms can facilitate language learning initiatives, share traditional stories and customs, and foster a sense of identity among younger generations.

Connect communities: Individuals dispersed geographically can connect and share cultural experiences, strengthening community bonds and fostering mutual support.

Resist cultural appropriation: Communities can take control of their narratives and representations, preventing their traditions from being misused or exploited.

Ultimately, the dark web presents a complex landscape for ethnic and cultural preservation. While harbouring risks and demanding responsible engagement, it offers a unique platform for empowering communities, safeguarding heritage, and bridging the digital divide for cultural survival. Approaching this realm with ethical considerations, community-driven initiatives, and a commitment to equitable access and legal compliance is crucial to harnessing its potential for positive impact and ensuring cultural heritage thrives in the digital age.

CHAPTER 60:
BEACONS OF HOPE: SUPPORT NETWORKS FOR IMMIGRANTS AND REFUGEES ON THE DARK WEB

Our final expedition on the dark web takes us to a realm driven by compassion and solidarity: support networks for immigrants and refugees. Imagine hidden pathways, not paved with data, but with whispered words of comfort, shared experiences, and vital information guiding vulnerable individuals navigating unfamiliar terrain. While acknowledging the ethical complexities and practical challenges, we delve into this shadowy space where digital anonymity empowers both those seeking support and those offering it.

Before venturing deeper, let us acknowledge the potential pitfalls. Anonymity, while protecting users' privacy, can hinder transparency and accountability. Malicious actors may exploit anonymity for misinformation, scams, or even human trafficking. It's crucial to approach such networks with caution, research platforms thoroughly, and verify information carefully.

Now, imagine the diverse motivations for seeking support on the dark web. Individuals facing persecution in their home countries, LGBTQ+ refugees fearing discrimination, or undocumented immigrants navigating complex legal systems might find safe havens in these anonymous online communities. They can connect with others who understand their struggles, share experiences, and access vital information on legal aid, safe passage routes, or resettlement opportunities.

Consider, for example, online forums offering legal advice and support to undocumented immigrants. In countries with restrictive immigration policies, such forums provide a lifeline for individuals navigating complex legal processes, offering emotional support, and connecting them with trusted legal resources. Similarly, LGBTQ+ refugees escaping persecution can connect with communities offering safe havens, cultural understanding, and emotional support in anonymous online spaces.

However, challenges abound beyond ethical considerations. Accessing the dark web requires technical expertise, and navigating its hidden spaces can be daunting for vulnerable populations. Additionally, verifying the legitimacy of platforms and users demands extra effort, making individuals susceptible to misinformation or exploitation.

Furthermore, legal complexities arise. While offering support and information might be legal in some regions, it might violate laws in others, putting both users and facilitators at risk. Legal awareness and responsible engagement remain crucial.

Despite the challenges, the potential for positive impact shines through. The dark web has empowered immigrants and refugees to:

Find and build communities: Individuals facing isolation and alienation can connect with others who share their experiences, fostering a sense of belonging and support.

Access vital information: Networks can offer legal resources, resettlement information, haven locations, and crucial knowledge about navigating new environments.

Share experiences and advocate for change: Individuals can connect with advocacy groups, share their stories, and raise awareness about the challenges faced by immigrants and refugees, contributing to positive social change.

Organize and mobilize: Online communities can facilitate communication and collaboration, enabling refugees to organize for their rights, advocate for better policies, and hold authorities accountable.

Ultimately, the dark web presents a complex landscape for immigrant and refugee support networks. While harbouring risks and demanding vigilance, it offers a unique platform for fostering solidarity, empowering individuals, and bridging information gaps. Approaching this realm with caution, meticulous research, and a commitment to responsible engagement is crucial to maximize its potential for positive impact and ensure vulnerable individuals find the support they need in the shadows.

PART XIII: FUTURE POTENTIAL

CHAPTER 61:
GLIMMERS OF LIGHT:
ADVANCEMENTS IN
TOR AND PRIVACY
TECHNOLOGIES

As we conclude our exploration of the good within the dark web, it's crucial to cast our gaze towards the future, where advancements in Tor and privacy technologies hold the potential to transform the digital landscape. Imagine the dark web not as a hidden alley, but as a blossoming field where anonymity empowers individuals, fosters innovation, and protects fundamental rights. While acknowledging the ongoing challenges and ethical considerations, we delve into the ongoing evolution of technologies that aim to safeguard privacy and create a more equitable digital world.

Before venturing deeper, let us address the complexities. While advancements in Tor and privacy technologies offer immense potential, their impact remains intertwined with broader societal and ethical considerations. Ensuring equitable access to these technologies across diverse communities is crucial to avoid exacerbating existing digital divides. Additionally, safeguarding against malicious actors exploiting anonymity for harmful purposes remains a constant challenge.

Balancing individual privacy with societal accountability and law enforcement needs necessitates ongoing dialogue and innovative solutions.

Now, imagine the transformative potential of these advancements. Decentralized networks like Tor and its successors aim to empower individuals by giving them control over their data and online presence. Imagine a future where anonymity becomes a fundamental right, enabling individuals to freely express themselves, access censored information, and organize for social change without fear of surveillance or persecution.

Consider, for example, the ongoing development of Onion Services v3, a promising upgrade to Tor's core infrastructure. This upgrade aims to improve performance, scalability, and resistance to potential attacks, further strengthening the anonymity and accessibility of the network. Additionally, projects like I2P and ZeroNet offer alternative decentralized architectures, fostering innovation and diversifying the options available for anonymous communication and information sharing.

However, challenges abound beyond ethical considerations. Ensuring user-friendliness and accessibility for less tech-savvy individuals remains crucial to bridging the digital divide and ensuring equitable access to privacy tools. Additionally, countering the potential misuse of anonymity for illegal activities requires collaborative efforts between technology developers, law enforcement agencies, and civil society organizations.

Furthermore, regulatory frameworks need to evolve alongside technological advancements. Striking a balance between protecting individual privacy and safeguarding against emerging threats requires nuanced, adaptable legal frameworks that prioritize human rights and responsible innovation.

Despite the challenges, the potential for positive impact shines through. Advancements in Tor and privacy technologies can:

Empower individuals: By giving individuals control over their data and online presence, these technologies enable them to exercise their right to privacy and engage in free expression without fear of reprisal.

Promote information access: Censorship-resistant tools can bridge information gaps, allowing individuals in oppressive regimes to access important news and resources otherwise unavailable.

Facilitate whistleblowing: Anonymity can empower individuals to expose wrongdoing and hold powerful entities accountable, contributing to transparency and good governance.

Foster innovation: Secure communication channels and decentralized platforms can stimulate the development of new technologies and innovative solutions to societal challenges.

Ultimately, the future of Tor and privacy technologies is intertwined with the broader evolution of the digital world. While harbouring challenges and demanding responsible development, these advancements offer a glimmer of hope for a future where individual privacy is respected, free expression flourishes, and technology empowers rather than enslaves. Approaching this future with ethical considerations, collaborative efforts, and a commitment to human rights is crucial to ensure the darkness of the unknown yields a future bathed in the light of innovation and individual empowerment.

CHAPTER 62: THE DIGITAL FRONTIER: EXPLORING EVOLVING ECONOMIES ON THE DARK WEB

Our exploration of the dark web culminates with a glimpse into its potential economic landscape. Imagine hidden pathways, not paved with data, but with whispers of alternative markets, decentralized currencies, and the nascent stirrings of a digital frontier. While acknowledging the inherent complexities and ethical considerations, we delve into the realm where anonymity fuels financial transactions, fosters innovation, and challenges traditional economic models.

Navigating the moral and practical maze: Before venturing deeper, let's recognize the ethical minefield. While some envision decentralized economies empowering individuals and breaking free from centralized control, others see fertile ground for illegal activities, money laundering, and exploitation. Understanding this duality is crucial. Engaging with these economies demands responsible action, awareness of legal frameworks, and prioritizing ethical use within established regulations.

Beyond currencies, a paradigm shift: Imagine the evolution of traditional financial systems with the emergence of cryptocurrencies like Bitcoin and Monero. These digital assets, often traded on the dark web, offer anonymity, decentralization, and potentially faster transactions. While raising concerns about financial regulation and potential misuse, they also fuel innovative forms of exchange and pave the way for alternative economic models.

Consider, for instance, Decentralized Autonomous Organizations (DAOs). These collective entities, governed by code and operating on blockchains, offer new models for crowdfunding, resource allocation, and even self-governing communities. Though nascent, DAOs have the potential to disrupt traditional economic structures and empower communities to manage their finances and investments.

However, challenges abound beyond ethical concerns. The anonymity offered by cryptocurrencies and dark web marketplaces can attract illegal activities, making it difficult to trace transactions and hold bad actors accountable. Additionally, technical complexities and volatility remain hurdles for widespread adoption and mainstream integration. Regulatory frameworks struggle to keep pace with the rapid evolution of this digital frontier.

Despite the challenges, the potential for positive impact shines through:

Financial inclusion: Individuals excluded from traditional financial systems due to geographical limitations or political repression can access alternative means of exchange and financial participation.

Empowering communities: DAOs and other decentralized models can empower communities to manage their resources, make collective decisions, and participate in a new wave of economic activity.

Transparency and accountability: Blockchain technology, upon which many of these systems are built, offers the potential for increased transparency and traceability in financial transactions, promoting accountability and reducing fraud.

Innovation and experimentation: The dark web acts as a breeding ground for innovative economic models and financial tools, challenging traditional approaches and potentially leading to more efficient and inclusive financial systems.

Ultimately, the future of the dark web's economic landscape remains uncertain. While harbouring risks and demanding responsible engagement, it offers a glimpse into a potential future where individuals have greater control over their finances, communities can operate autonomously, and innovation disrupts traditional economic models. Approaching this future with an awareness of ethical considerations, a commitment to regulatory compliance, and a focus on positive social impact is crucial to ensure that the digital frontier unlocks economic possibilities for all.

CHAPTER 63: WHISPERS OF CHANGE: THE FUTURE OF DIGITAL ACTIVISM ON THE DARK WEB

As we conclude our odyssey through the shadows, we arrive at a crucial crossroads: the evolving role of the dark web in digital activism. Imagine a hidden network, not paved with data, but with whispers of dissent, coordinated campaigns, and a digital backbone for social change. While acknowledging the inherent complexities and ethical considerations, we delve into the future of activism, where anonymity empowers movements, fosters innovation, and challenges the status quo.

Before venturing deeper, let us acknowledge the ethical maze. While anonymity fuels dissent in oppressive regimes and protects sensitive information, it can also shield malicious actors and hinder accountability. Navigating this space requires responsible engagement, prioritizing ethical use, and ensuring actions align with established human rights principles. Remember, the fight for justice cannot justify harming others or violating ethical boundaries.

Now, imagine the potential for transformative action. In countries with restricted freedoms, the dark web offers a platform for organizing protests, sharing censored information, and coordinating resistance movements. Activists can bypass state surveillance, connect with international supporters, and amplify their voices beyond the reach of censorship.

Consider, for instance, the use of dark web forums by activists in authoritarian regimes. These hidden platforms facilitate communication, resource sharing, and even secure training sessions, empowering individuals to organize and challenge oppressive systems. Similarly, whistle-blowers can anonymously leak sensitive information on human rights abuses or government corruption, sparking investigations and holding authorities accountable.

However, challenges abound beyond ethical concerns. Technical barriers like access and digital literacy can limit participation, particularly in marginalized communities. Additionally, verifying information shared on the dark web can be difficult, making it susceptible to misinformation and manipulation. Furthermore, navigating complex legal frameworks and avoiding unintended consequences remains crucial for responsible activism.

Despite the challenges, the potential for positive impact remains significant:

Empowering marginalized voices: The dark web can provide a haven for activists facing persecution, enabling them to organize, share experiences, and advocate for their rights without fear of reprisal.

Facilitating international collaboration: Activists worldwide can connect, share best practices, and coordinate efforts across borders, amplifying their impact and mobilizing international support.

Promoting transparency and accountability: Anonymous whistleblowing can expose human rights abuses and corruption, leading to investigations and holding powerful actors accountable.

Developing innovative tools and strategies: The dark web fosters experimentation and innovation, leading to the development of new tools for secure communication, data encryption, and online mobilization techniques.

Ultimately, the future of digital activism on the dark web is as uncertain as the future of the dark web itself. While harbouring risks and demanding responsible engagement, it offers a platform for amplifying marginalized voices, challenging unjust systems, and fostering international solidarity. Approaching this future with an awareness of ethical considerations, a commitment to legal compliance, and a focus on collective action is crucial to ensuring that the shadows become a breeding ground for positive change and social justice.

CHAPTER 64: UNCHARTED TERRITORY: ETHICAL DEBATES AND THE NEXT GENERATION OF THE DARK WEB

Our expedition through the hidden corners of the web concludes not with a definitive answer but with an invitation to participate in an ongoing conversation. As the dark web evolves, so too do the ethical questions surrounding its existence and potential. Imagine the hidden network not as a static map, but as a dynamic landscape where new technologies, challenges, and opportunities emerge, demanding thoughtful consideration from the next generation.

Navigating the ethical labyrinth: Before venturing deeper, let us acknowledge the complex ethical terrain. While acknowledging the potential for good explored in previous chapters, ethical concerns remain pervasive. Issues like privacy vs. accountability, anonymity vs. exploitation, and freedom of expression vs. harmful content require ongoing dialogue and nuanced solutions. Engaging in this conversation involves critical thinking, understanding diverse perspectives, and embracing the responsibility to shape the future of the dark web ethically.

Now, imagine the new frontiers emerging at the intersection of technology and the dark web. Artificial intelligence, blockchain technology, and decentralized platforms pave the way for an even more complex and potentially transformative digital landscape. While offering opportunities for privacy-enhancing technologies, secure communication, and innovative solutions, these advancements also raise questions about potential biases, algorithmic discrimination, and the concentration of power in the hands of tech giants.

Consider, for instance, the ethical implications of AI-powered surveillance tools used on the dark web. While potentially aiding in the fight against illegal activities, such tools might infringe on individual privacy and exacerbate existing inequalities. Similarly, the use of blockchain technology in the dark web raises questions about anonymity and accountability, as transactions might be untraceable while simultaneously empowering illicit actors.

However, challenges also pave the way for creative solutions. Ethical AI development, decentralized governance models, and community-driven initiatives can help mitigate risks and ensure that the dark web becomes a force for good. Fostering open dialogue, collaboration between stakeholders, and responsible innovation are crucial in shaping the ethical future of this digital frontier.

Debates worthy of our time: As we hand the torch to the next generation, here are some vital questions to consider:

Balancing privacy with accountability: How can we guarantee privacy for individuals while holding bad actors accountable, ensuring the dark web doesn't become a haven for illegal activities?

Empowering users vs. protecting vulnerable individuals: How

can we empower users with knowledge and tools to navigate the dark web safely and ethically while protecting vulnerable individuals from exploitation and misinformation?

Innovation with ethical boundaries: How can we promote responsible innovation on the dark web, ensuring new technologies enhance privacy and freedom without infringing on human rights or exacerbating existing inequalities?

Global collaboration vs. national interests: How can we foster international collaboration to regulate the dark web ethically while respecting diverse national interests and cultural backgrounds?

Ultimately, the future of the dark web lies not in our hands alone, but in the hands of the next generation. By equipping them with knowledge, critical thinking skills, and a commitment to ethical responsibility, we can ensure that the hidden corners of the web become a catalyst for positive change, empowering individuals, fostering innovation, and shaping a more just and equitable digital future for all.

CHAPTER 65:
CULTIVATING LIGHT:
EXPANDING THE
POSITIVE ASPECTS
OF THE DARK WEB

As we conclude our exploration of the good within the dark web, it's not enough to simply acknowledge its potential. We must actively cultivate this potential, nurturing the seeds of hope and expanding the positive aspects of this hidden digital landscape. Imagine the dark web not as a static map, but as a fertile field awaiting cultivation, where collaboration, innovation, and responsible engagement can yield a harvest of positive impact.

Before venturing deeper, let us acknowledge the challenges hindering its growth. While acknowledging the positive stories explored in previous chapters, the shadows still harbour risks. Lack of accessibility, technical barriers, and ethical concerns remain hurdles to wider adoption and responsible use. Addressing these challenges requires collaborative efforts, educational initiatives, and a commitment to ethical development.

Now, imagine the blossoming potential waiting to be cultivated. The dark web offers a unique platform for:

Empowering marginalized communities: Individuals facing repression, discrimination, or censorship can find safe spaces for communication, organization, and advocacy.

Facilitating whistleblowing and accountability: Anonymity empowers individuals to expose wrongdoing and hold powerful entities accountable, fostering transparency and good governance.

Fuelling innovation and experimentation: Decentralized platforms and privacy-enhancing technologies encourage the development of new solutions for communication, data security, and online activities.

Preserving knowledge and cultural heritage: Endangered languages, traditional knowledge, and artistic expressions can be anonymously documented and shared, safeguarding them for future generations.

While these possibilities are promising, cultivating them requires specific actions:

Bridging the digital divide: Educational initiatives and community-driven projects can equip individuals with the skills and knowledge needed to safely and ethically, navigate the dark web.

Promoting responsible development: Technology developers, researchers, and ethical hackers must collaborate to ensure new tools and platforms on the dark web prioritize privacy, security, and user wellbeing.

Fostering collaborative governance: International cooperation and multi-stakeholder dialogues are crucial to establishing ethical frameworks and regulations for the dark web, balancing individual rights with societal needs.

Prioritizing ethical engagement: Users must approach the dark web with caution, critical thinking, and a commitment to ethical use, avoiding illegal activities and harmful content.

Remember, the dark web is not a magic solution, but a tool with its complexities. Just as a field requires careful tending to yield its potential, harnessing the good within the dark web demands ongoing effort, collaboration, and responsible engagement. Here are some key areas for future exploration:

Decentralized social networks: Can we create censorship-resistant platforms for free expression and community building while mitigating the spread of misinformation and harmful content?

Privacy-enhancing technologies: Can we develop new tools for secure communication, data encryption, and anonymity that empower individuals without compromising accountability?

Collaborative knowledge sharing: Can we build secure platforms for researchers, activists, and marginalized communities to share information and resources across borders?

Ethical AI development: Can we ensure that artificial intelligence deployed on the dark web upholds ethical principles, avoids bias, and protects human rights?

Ultimately, the future of the good on the dark web is not predetermined. It's a story yet to be written, a collaborative effort where individuals, developers, policymakers, and civil society organizations join hands to cultivate a more equitable, ethical, and empowering digital landscape. By nurturing the seeds of potential and tending to the challenges, we can ensure the dark web blossoms into a force for good, illuminating the path towards a brighter digital future for all.

PART XIV: PERSONAL STORIES

CHAPTER 66: WHISPERS IN THE DARKNESS: AN ACTIVIST'S DIARY - A LIFE SAVED BY THE DARK WEB

June 12, 2022: Fear is a constant companion here. The oppressive regime's eyes are everywhere, searching for dissent, silencing any voice raised against their tyranny. My activism, once a beacon of hope for our community, is now a target painted on my back. Today, I received a chilling message - a warning to disappear or face the consequences. Panic threatened to consume me, but then, a lifeline emerged from the shadows: the dark web.

June 15, 2022: Navigating the hidden corners of the web felt like venturing into a clandestine world. Anonymity cloaked me, offering a sense of security I hadn't felt in months. With trembling fingers, I typed my desperate plea for help on a secure forum frequented by activists. Within hours, messages of support and guidance flooded my screen. They offered escape routes, secure communication channels, and even digital tools to protect my identity. Hope, a flicker I thought extinguished, reignited within me.

June 20, 2022: The escape was harrowing. Guided by anonymous instructions, I slipped through back alleys, evaded checkpoints, and finally crossed the border into a land where dissent wasn't a crime. The dark web had saved my life, but the journey wasn't over. My voice, though silenced in my homeland, could still resonate online.

July 10, 2022: From my newfound sanctuary, I joined a network of exiled activists on the dark web. We shared stories, strategized resistance movements, and amplified the plight of those still trapped under the regime's thumb. The anonymity this platform offered allowed us to connect with international supporters, bypassing government censorship and exposing the truth to the world.

August 5, 2022: The dark web wasn't just a shield; it became a sword. Using secure communication channels, we coordinated peaceful protests, organized boycotts, and leaked incriminating documents exposing the regime's abuses. The impact was undeniable. Our voices, once whispered in the dark, started echoing through the streets, igniting a spark of defiance within our homeland.

September 22, 2022: Today, news reached me: the regime crumbled. The people, empowered by our online resistance, rose, and demanded change. Tears streamed down my face, a mixture of grief for what I lost and joy for what we achieved. The dark web, a place of shadows, had birthed light, proving that even in the darkest corners, hope and courage can bloom.

October 15, 2022: Though I yearn to return home, the fight isn't over. The road to rebuilding a just society is long and arduous. But now, I stand with my people, not in the shadows, but in the open, using the lessons learned in the dark web to advocate for transparency, accountability, and a future where dissent is not silenced, but celebrated.

This is just one story, a testament to the potential for good within the dark web. While ethical concerns and risks remain, it can empower the marginalized, offer a platform for whistleblowing, and foster collaboration for positive change. As with any tool, its impact depends on the hands that wield it. Let us strive to ensure those hands are guided by ethical principles, a commitment to justice, and the unwavering belief that even in the darkest corners, light can prevail.

CHAPTER 67: FROM SCEPTIC TO USER: A JOURNALIST'S JOURNEY INTO THE HEART OF THE DARK WEB

My journey into the dark web began, like many others, with scepticism. Whispers of illegal marketplaces, nefarious activities, and shadowy figures filled the narrative. Curiosity, however, gnawed at the edges of my cynicism. Could there be more to this hidden internet than sensationalized headlines proclaimed? With a mix of apprehension and intrigue, I ventured into the unknown, my journalistic spirit urging me to explore the potential stories tucked away in the darkness.

This expedition wasn't a plunge into the abyss. Instead, it was a gradual descent, guided by trusted sources and meticulous research. I learned the language of anonymity, navigated encrypted pathways, and delved into forums buzzing with diverse voices. As I shed my preconceived notions, a different picture emerged.

Beyond Illegality: A Mosaic of Needs and Voices

While illegal activities undoubtedly exist on the dark web, they only scratched the surface of the complex ecosystem I encountered. My initial shock at finding support groups for marginalized communities, platforms for whistle-blowers to expose corruption, and libraries safeguarding endangered cultural heritage quickly replaced my scepticism. Here, individuals facing oppression, censorship, and discrimination found safe havens for communication, organization, and advocacy.

Case Study: The Silenced Speaks

Take, for instance, my interaction with "Ghost", a pseudonym used by a journalist from a repressive regime. In his home country, sharing critical information meant imprisonment. On the dark web, he anonymously published investigative reports, exposing human rights abuses and government corruption. His work, disseminated through secure channels, ignited dialogues, and empowered citizens to demand accountability. Ghost's story, one of many, illustrated the dark web's potential to amplify silenced voices and promote transparency in the face of oppression.

Ethical Quandaries: Walking a Tightrope

Yet, navigating the grey areas remained a constant challenge. The anonymity that empowers also harbours malicious actors. Countering misinformation, verifying information sources, and ensuring ethical engagement became crucial skills. Collaboration with other researchers, ethical hackers, and journalists proved invaluable in navigating the ethical labyrinth and ensuring responsible reporting.

A Force for Good, Used Responsibly

My journey taught me that the dark web is not inherently good or bad. It's a tool, and like any tool, its impact depends on the user. When wielded responsibly, it can be a powerful force for positive change. Whistle-blowers can expose wrongdoing, activists can organize resistance, and individuals facing persecution can find support and community.

However, this potential comes with immense responsibility. Users must be aware of the ethical considerations, navigate with caution, and prioritize legal compliance. Journalists venturing into the dark web must uphold ethical journalistic principles, ensuring source verification, fact-checking, and responsible reporting.

The Future: Collaboration and Responsible Innovation

As the dark web evolves, so must our understanding and engagement. Continued research, collaboration between stakeholders, and the development of ethical frameworks are crucial to harnessing its potential for good while mitigating risks. Governments, technology developers, civil society organizations, and users alike must work together to ensure this hidden space becomes a catalyst for positive change, promoting individual empowerment, fostering innovation, and safeguarding fundamental rights in the digital age.

My journey is not over. The dark web remains a complex and ever-evolving landscape. But as I move forward, I carry the lessons learned: critical thinking, responsible engagement, and the belief that even in the darkest corners, the potential for good exists, waiting to be discovered and nurtured.

CHAPTER 68: THE TALE OF A DARK WEB SAMARITAN: HOPE IN THE SHADOWS

The dark web, often shrouded in mystery and negativity, holds unexpected stories of compassion and humanity. This chapter delves into the tale of "Nightingale," a pseudonym for a hidden figure who embodies the potential for good within the digital shadows.

A Beacon in the Darkness: Nightingale's story began in a hidden forum frequented by individuals facing persecution and repression. Here, amidst discussions of survival and escape routes, Nightingale emerged as a beacon of hope. Utilizing their technical expertise, they offered anonymous guidance and support to those seeking refuge.

Beyond Borders, Beyond Risks: Nightingale's assistance transcended geographical boundaries. They helped individuals navigate complex legal systems, connect with safe havens across the globe, and even provided financial aid through secure cryptocurrency transactions. However, their actions weren't without risks. Operating in the dark web's grey areas demanded constant vigilance and awareness of potential dangers.

A Web of Trust, Woven with Caution: Building trust in a space notorious for anonymity was no small feat. Nightingale earned the respect of the community through consistent, reliable support, meticulous attention to detail, and a genuine desire to help. Their actions spoke louder than words, creating a ripple effect of hope and gratitude within the forum.

The Cost of Compassion: But Nightingale's story isn't just about selfless acts. The emotional toll of witnessing suffering and navigating the dark web's complexities was significant. The constant fear of exposure, the ethical dilemmas of navigating legal boundaries, and the emotional investment in each individual's journey took their toll.

The Butterfly Effect: A Ripple of Change: Despite the challenges, Nightingale's impact was undeniable. Individuals who once felt lost and alone found safe havens, rebuilt their lives, and even became active members of their new communities. The ripple effect of their actions extended beyond the immediate beneficiaries, inspiring others to offer support and fostering a sense of solidarity within the forum.

A Call to Action: Beyond Nightingale's Story: Nightingale's tale is a reminder that the dark web, while harbouring risks, also holds the potential for good. It serves as a call to action for individuals and organizations to engage responsibly with this complex digital space.

Promoting ethical use: Awareness campaigns and educational initiatives can help users navigate the dark web safely and ethically.
Empowering communities: Building platforms and resources within the dark web can empower marginalized communities to connect, share information, and advocate for their rights.
Fostering collaboration: Collaboration between law enforcement, technology developers, and civil society organizations is crucial to addressing illegal activities while safeguarding individual rights and fostering responsible

innovation.

The Future of the Dark Web: A Collective Responsibility: The future of the dark web remains uncertain. Yet, Nightingale's story demonstrates that even in the darkest corners, individuals can choose to be forces for good. As we move forward, let us remember that shaping the future of this digital space requires a collective effort, guided by ethical principles, a commitment to human rights, and a belief in the potential for good that lies within even the most unexpected places.

CHAPTER 69: HOPE IN THE SHADOWS: A WHISTLE-BLOWER'S CHRONICLE

The shadows held my story, a tale not meant for the bright glare of the public eye. Yet, my silence felt like a betrayal, a complicit nod to the injustices unfolding within the walls of the powerful institution I once served. The dark web whispered about in hushed tones, emerged as my unlikely confidante, a platform where shadows could speak and truth could find shelter.

A Breach of Trust, A Spark of Courage: My decision wasn't impulsive. Witnessing wrongdoing, its tendrils reaching far and wide had gnawed at my conscience for months. Reporting internally felt futile, lost in a labyrinth of bureaucracy and self-preservation. The dark web, with its cloak of anonymity and potential for international reach, became my last resort.

Navigating the Labyrinth of Anonymity: Venturing into this hidden digital space was akin to entering a labyrinth. Learning the language of encryption, accessing secure forums, and verifying information demanded meticulous caution. But fear was a luxury I couldn't afford. Every step, every message sent, carried the weight of potential exposure and consequences.

Sharing the Burden, Amplifying the Message: Within the

shadows, I found community. Others, driven by similar motives, offered guidance and support. Journalists, activists, and fellow whistle-blowers formed a safety net, vetting information, amplifying my story, and ensuring it reached the right ears. The dark web, often demonized, became a platform for collaboration, a space where isolated voices could unite and amplify their message.

The Price of Truth: Living in the Shadows: My act of whistleblowing sparked a ripple effect. Investigations were launched, reforms initiated, and accountability sought. Yet, the personal cost was significant. The constant fear of retaliation, social isolation, and the burden of potential harm to loved ones became my unwelcome companions. Living in the shadows, once a shield, morphed into a cage, a constant reminder of the sacrifices made for truth.

Beyond the Shadows: A Call to Action: My story is not unique. Countless individuals navigate the dark web, seeking justice, exposing corruption, and fighting for a better world. While ethical concerns and risks abound, we cannot ignore the potential for good it holds.

Protecting whistle-blowers: Robust legal frameworks and ethical guidelines are crucial to protect whistle-blowers, regardless of the platform they utilize.
Empowering responsible journalism: Investigative journalists require access to secure technologies and resources to navigate the dark web responsibly and ethically.
Fostering global collaboration: International cooperation is vital to address criminal activities while safeguarding individual rights and promoting responsible innovation.

From Shadows to Sunlight: Shaping the Future: The dark web remains an enigma, a complex ecosystem with the potential for both harm and good. Our approach cannot be one of fear or demonization but of understanding, responsible engagement, and ethical innovation. It is our collective responsibility to ensure that the shadows become not breeding grounds for darkness, but a platform for amplifying marginalized voices, exposing injustices, and ultimately, shaping a more just and equitable future for all.

CHAPTER 70: A VISIONARY'S DREAM: WEAVING LIGHT INTO THE DARK WEB TAPESTRY

As we conclude our exploration of the good within the dark web, it's not enough to simply acknowledge its potential. We must envision a future where this hidden digital space transcends its shadows, becoming a beacon of good, woven into the tapestry of the internet with purpose and ethical foundations. Imagine a dark web not driven by anonymity alone but by a collective commitment to social progress, justice, and empowerment.

Bridging the Divide: From Shadows to Transparency

The dark web's anonymity, while crucial for many seeking refuge or exposing wrongdoing, can also hinder accountability and transparency. Can we find solutions that prioritize privacy while enabling responsible actors to be identified and held accountable? Decentralized identity management systems, reputation frameworks within secure communities, and responsible whistleblowing mechanisms are possibilities worth exploring.

Empowering Communities: Beyond Borders, Beyond Censorship

The dark web has empowered marginalized communities facing oppression and censorship. Can we expand this potential, fostering platforms for cultural exchange, knowledge sharing, and collective action, while ensuring accessibility and bridging the digital divide across regions and demographics? Educational initiatives, secure communication tools, and decentralized governance models can play a crucial role in making this vision a reality.

Innovation with Ethics: Harnessing Technology for Good

Technologies like blockchain and artificial intelligence, often associated with the dark web, hold immense potential for good. Can we develop and deploy these technologies ethically on the dark web, tackling challenges like misinformation, bias, and algorithmic discrimination while harnessing their potential for secure communication, data protection, and decentralized governance? Fostering collaboration between developers, researchers, and civil society organizations is key to achieving this balance.

Global Collaboration: Uniting for a Shared Future

The dark web transcends national borders. Can we foster international cooperation and dialogue to establish ethical frameworks, address illegal activities, and promote responsible innovation in this shared digital space? Collaborative research, multi-stakeholder forums, and international treaties can guide us towards a future where the dark web operates within a global framework that respects human rights and promotes shared prosperity.

A Responsibility of All: Shaping the Future Together

This visionary dream cannot be realized by a select few. It requires the collective responsibility of individual users, technology developers, governments, and civil society organizations. Here are some key areas for action:

Individual engagement: Users must approach the dark web with critical thinking, ethical considerations, and a commitment to responsible use.

Tech development: Developers must prioritize privacy, security, and ethical principles when designing tools and platforms for the dark web.

Policy frameworks: Governments need to collaborate on regulations that balance individual rights with societal needs, addressing illegal activities without stifling innovation.

Civil society advocacy: Organizations can promote responsible engagement, hold stakeholders accountable, and ensure the dark web contributes to a more equitable and just digital future.

CONCLUSION:

The Dual Nature of Technology: Harnessing the Positive Potential of the Dark Web

Our expedition through the shadows has come to an end. We've explored the hidden corners of the dark web, uncovering not just its dangers and ethical complexities, but also its surprising potential for good. From empowering marginalized voices to facilitating whistleblowing and fostering innovation, the stories we've encountered paint a nuanced picture of technology often vilified.

The Duality of the Digital World:

Technology, like the dark web itself, is neither inherently good nor bad. It's a tool, a double-edged sword whose impact depends on the hands that wield it. Just as a scalpel can save lives or inflict harm, the dark web can be a platform for oppression or a haven for liberation, depending on our choices and actions.

Embracing the Potential, Mitigating the Risks:

Ignoring the dark web's potential for good would be a missed opportunity. By acknowledging its risks and navigating its complexities with ethical considerations in mind, we can harness its potential to improve lives and create a more just and equitable digital future.

Key Learnings from Our Exploration:

The dark web is not a monolith. It's a diverse ecosystem with a spectrum of activities, both legal and illegal, ethical, and unethical. Generalizing about it is like judging an entire forest based on a single rotten apple.

Anonymity can be a double-edged sword. While it empowers vulnerable individuals and facilitates whistleblowing, it can also shield malicious actors. Finding the right balance between privacy and accountability is crucial.

Responsible engagement is paramount. Individuals venturing into the dark web must prioritize responsible use, critical thinking, and awareness of legal and ethical frameworks.

Collaboration is key. Stakeholders ranging from users and developers to researchers, policymakers, and civil society organizations must work together to address challenges, promote responsible innovation, and shape the future of the dark web.

A Call to Action: Shaping the Future Together

As we move forward, let us remember that the future of the dark web is not predetermined. It lies in our hands, shaped by the choices we make and the actions we take. Here are some key areas for action:

Individual responsibility: Each user must approach the dark web with caution, critical thinking, and a commitment to ethical engagement.

Technological development: Developers must prioritize privacy, security, and ethical principles when designing tools and platforms for the dark web.

Policy frameworks: Governments need to collaborate on regulations that balance individual rights with societal needs, addressing illegal activities without hindering innovation.

Civil society engagement: Organizations can promote responsible use, hold stakeholders accountable, and advocate for policies that ensure the dark web contributes to a more equitable and just digital future.

The dark web remains an enigma, a complex digital space

demanding ongoing exploration and responsible engagement. While challenges and ethical concerns persist, let us not overlook the potential for good it holds. By working together, fostering responsible innovation, and prioritizing ethical principles, we can ensure that the shadows become not a breeding ground for darkness, but a platform for positive change, illuminating the path towards a brighter digital future for all.

DISCLAIMER FOR "THE GOOD ON THE DARK WEB"

This book explores the potential positive aspects of the dark web, highlighting stories and possibilities that often go unnoticed. However, it is crucial to understand and acknowledge the inherent risks and ethical complexities associated with this hidden digital space. The dark web also harbours illegal activities, malicious actors, and potential dangers that demand caution and responsible engagement.

This book does not:

Endorse or encourage any illegal or unethical activities on the dark web.
Provide instructions or guides for navigating the dark web.
Minimize the risks associated with dark web engagement.
Condone or promote any specific individuals or groups operating on the dark web.

Before venturing into the dark web, it is essential to:

Educate yourself about the legal and ethical considerations involved.
Understand the potential risks, including malware, scams, and illegal content.
Take appropriate security measures to protect your privacy and data.

THE GOOD ON THE DARK WEB

Only access the dark web through trusted and secure connections.
Avoid engaging in any illegal or unethical activities.

This book serves as an informational resource and does not replace individual responsibility and due diligence. Remember, the decision to access the dark web and the actions you take within it are ultimately yours.

Please proceed with caution, prioritize safety and ethical use, and never engage in activities that violate the law or compromise your well-being.

www.ingramcontent.com/pod-product-compliance
Lightning Source LLC
LaVergne TN
LVHW051732050326
832903LV00023B/897